This life is filled with struggles. Our faith in Christ does not exempt us from these difficulties—at times it actually exacerbates them! But thankfully in Christ we have a hope and a strength that supersedes life's struggles. Philip De Courcy skillfully delivers the spiritual tools and biblical perspective we need to keep first things first as we encounter our daily challenges. *Emergency Rations* is the kind of book you can pick up and read five minutes at a time. These brief, challenging, and encouraging nuggets of truth will fortify your faith and spur you on to face each day with boldness to live for Christ.

Mike Fabarez,
Pastor, Compass Bible Church, Aliso Viejo, California
Author of *Lifelines for Tough Times*

Philip De Courcy, my friend and former pastor, has written a very helpful devotional tool. As we face challenging circumstances in life and are tempted to focus on those challenges, Pastor Philip provides each believer a source for great potential encouragement. These devotional insights point the reader in the right direction, to our great and good God. His insights are consistently biblical, relevant, and interesting.

Michael A. Grisanti,
Professor of Old Testament,
The Master's Seminary, Sun Valley, California

In the book of Psalms we read of God giving songs in the night. In this book my friend and bible teacher Philip De Courcy serves up some bite size truths that will help you survive the tough times with your joy intact. Read it and rejoice anew in the love of God and the grace of our Lord Jesus Christ!

Keith Getty,
Christian artist and modern hymn writer

Pastor Philip De Courcy is highly respected in his homeland of Ireland as an excellent Bible expositor of God's Word. It gives me great joy to commend *Emergency Rations* for your favorable consideration. You'll find the content to be similar in style to his teaching, theologically robust, illustratively helpful and practically accessible. My hope is that this collection of devotions might encourage you to discover the "unsearchable riches of Christ.

Freddie McClaughlin
President, Baptist Association in Ireland

With one hundred splendid devotionals, which treat fourteen kinds of life struggles common to Christians worldwide, Pastor Philip De Courcy skillfully dispenses biblically-based, practically-illustrated, and eternally-wise counsel by which to survive these difficulties. *Emergency Rations* should be on every Christian's spiritual pantry shelf.

Richard Mayhue,
Research Professor of Theology Emeritus,
The Master's Seminary, Sun Valley, California

EMERGENCY RATIONS

SURVIVING THE STRUGGLES OF LIFE

PHILIP DE COURCY

CHRISTIAN
FOCUS

Philip De Courcy has been the Senior Pastor of Kindred Community Church in Anaheim Hills, California since 2007. He also broadcasts sermons on Know The Truth, a radio program.

Copyright © Philip De Courcy 2017

paperback ISBN 978-1-78191-968-2
epub ISBN 978-1-78191-991-0
mobi ISBN 978-1-78191-992-7

10 9 8 7 6 5 4 3 2 1

Published in 2017
by
Christian Focus Publications, Ltd.
Geanies House, Fearn,
Ross-shire, IV20 1TW, Scotland.
www.christianfocus.com

Cover design by Pete Barnsley

Printed by Bell & Bain, Glasgow

MIX
Paper from
responsible sources
FSC® C007785

CONTENTS

Dedication

To George and Anna Sanders thank you for your friendship,
support and Christian love from the time
the De Courcy's arrived in America to the present.
You are undoubtedly a good and perfect gift
from our Father in heaven.

Preface

As someone who lives in California, and who has lived through some of its earthquakes the prospect, and thought of the next big one is, frighteningly, never far away. That is why federal and state agencies recommend to citizens like myself that we stockpile some Emergency Rations. Items such as water, non-perishable food, a first-aid kit, dust masks, flashlights, a whistle to signal for help, cell phones with chargers, and warm blankets just to name a few. Like good Boy Scouts the residents of California always need to be prepared for their worlds to be shaken.

Just like with an earthquake in California our personal world's can suddenly be shaken by a bad doctor's report, a moral failure, a spiritual dry spell, a financial collapse, a cruel betrayal or a mystifying providence. This book has been written to provide you with some Emergency Rations to help you survive the struggles of life. Here you will find bite size theology that I trust will promote your spiritual health and holiness during times of trial and temptation. I hope you will keep this book near at hand, and reach for it during life's tremors, and find strength for today and bright hope for tomorrow.

Philip De Courcy
California 2016

Surviving
the Struggle to Understand God's Purposes in Our Circumstances

Leave it Alone

Then the king said to Zadok, 'Carry the ark of God back into the city. If I find favor in the eyes of the LORD, He will bring me back and show me both it and His dwelling place. But if He says thus: "I have no delight in you," here I am, let Him do to me as seems good to Him.'

(2 SAMUEL 15:25-6)

One of the great challenges and choices in life when faced with overwhelming trouble is to take things into our own hands or leave them in God's hands. In life we can find ourselves in a moment of crisis, standing at a fork in the road, having to consciously decide between trusting ourselves and resting in God's sovereignty. At that moment, the wise man or woman realizes it is best to leave things with God.

In 2 Samuel 15, we find King David having to flee the city of Jerusalem in the face of his own son's treachery. Absalom had stolen the hearts of the citizenry, turned them against his father, and was marching against Jerusalem. In the face of Absalom's advance, David withdraws to avoid the bloodbath of a prolonged siege. Insult is added to injury as David learns that his trusted friend and wise counselor, Ahithophel, had betrayed him. He is also told that Mephibosheth, to whom he had shown great kindness, was also among the scoundrels who had conspired against him.

In the midst of this chaos and crisis, David does something interesting and inspiring. For the sake of the people, the king does a noble thing and sends Zadok, his beloved priest and faithful friend, back to Jerusalem with the Ark of the Covenant (2 Sam. 15:25-6). David surmises that if it was God's will for him to return as king, he would do so. Hence there was no need to keep the Ark of the Covenant away from the sanctuary. The royal fugitive muses: 'If I find favor in the eyes of the Lord, He will bring me back and show me both it and His dwelling place.' If not, 'Let Him do to me as it seems good to Him.' David doesn't take things into his own hands. He leaves things in God's hands.

Perhaps, like David, your life is in a tailspin. Things are out of control in your body, your home, your business, and your ministry. Your future is out of your hands, and in someone else's hands. You feel vulnerable and exposed. You want to do something – anything – but your choices are limited. You want to act, but you fear doing the wrong thing, only making matters worse.

If that describes you, remember that even if power has been wrested from your hands, your times are in God's hands (Ps. 31:15). Nothing happens to you except by the will of God. Your emergency is in God's hands. Your enemy is in God's hands. In the midst of your losses, don't lose your confidence in the sovereignty of God. What seems good to Him is ultimately good for us (Rom. 8:28). Some years ago, I read something that Warren Wiersbe said, and it has stuck with me and served me well. He said: 'God gives his best to those who leave the choice to Him.' Best leave it to God.

God, whatever I leave with You is safe.
Help me to entrust myself to You.
In Jesus' Name, amen.

It's All Good

And we know that all things work together for good to those who love God, to those who are the called according to his purpose.

(ROMANS 8:28)

I have a friend in ministry who has a wonderful habit of invariably finishing a conversation, especially when talking of difficult problems or people, with the phrase, 'It is all good.' His words are based on the wonderful promise in Romans 8:28 where those loved by God are reminded that He is actively working *all* things in their lives together for their good. That little word *all* makes a big difference, doesn't it?

Temptation, grief, monetary loss, indecision, persecution, and sickness are not good things in themselves. But God orchestrates our lives in such a way that they prove beneficial both temporally and eternally. Good must be defined on God's terms, not ours, and is fundamentally tied to that which enhances our reliance upon God and our likeness to Christ. Depending on Christ and developing into His likeness *is* our greatest good, by the way. After all, God's goal is to bring us to perfection in His presence (Rom. 8:29; Eph. 5:27; Jude 24), which is bigger and better than our earthly ideas of good.

The message from Romans 8:28, then, is that there is nothing outside the scope of our heavenly Father's providential care that can touch or threaten our lives. Absolutely nothing! Even the bad can be good for us, as Joseph lived to learn (Gen. 50:20). By faith we must come to see that in the end our troubles are nothing but severe mercies.

The late Reformed theologian John Gerstner said there were four categories of things. First, there is the *good good*, which speaks of those things that conform to God's law both in action and motive. Second, there is the *bad good*, which speaks of righteous actions that are animated by impure motives. Third, there is the *bad bad*, which speaks of unmitigated evil. Fourth, there is the *good bad*, which speaks of things that do not conform to God's law or perfect will but are redeemed nonetheless in the providence of God.

We are talking about God's ability to bring good out of the evil we experience. The bad things remain bad, but they are only proximately bad because God is able to turn them, over time, into blessings in disguise.

There is always an upside to down in God's kingdom. That is why the end of a thing can be better than the beginning for the Christian (Eccles. 7:8). Therefore, let us cultivate patience in the midst of our trials, knowing that God is actively working on our behalf to bring us to a better day (Rom. 5:3-5). Give God time to move us beyond the times we are in to better times (Eccles. 3:11). Above all, we must give God our trust and fight the temptation to question His goodness (Job 13:15).

C. H. Spurgeon once said: 'Everything that happens to you is for your own good ... You gain by loss, you grow healthy in sickness, you live by dying, and you are made rich in losses ... It is better that all things should work for my good than all things should be as I wish to have them.'

Every cloud is silver-lined with God's providence. Remember, it's all good!

God, You are sovereign.
So, give me eyes to see even the good bad.
In Jesus' Name, amen.

All's Well That Ends Well

Then the seventh angel sounded: And there were loud voices in heaven, saying, 'The kingdoms of this world have become the kingdoms of our Lord and of his Christ, and he shall reign forever and ever!'

(REVELATION 11:15)

A janitor would wait patiently each week for a group of seminarians to finish their basketball game before cleaning the gym. While he waited, he would sit in the stands and study his Bible. One particular day, as the seminarians were exiting the gym, they noticed the janitor engrossed in Bible study. One of the young budding pastors asked which biblical book the janitor was studying. The old man answered, 'The book of Revelation.' The ball player was surprised and further asked the janitor if he understood the complicated book. 'Oh, yes,' the man replied, 'I understand it. It means that in the end Jesus wins!'

That is a great answer and an accurate analysis of the book of Revelation. It has been well said that the books of Genesis and Revelation act as two bookends that hold the entire Bible together. In Genesis we have the story of man's fall into sin, while in Revelation we have God's complete and final victory over sin (Rev. 11:15-18; 12:10-12; 19:11-16; 20:1-6). As the Alpha and Omega – the First and the Last – God in Christ restores His rule, and returns the earth to its original design (Rev. 21:6; 22:13). In the beginning Satan deceives humanity, but in the end he is bound to keep him from deceiving the nations (Gen. 3:1-7, 13-15; Rev. 20:2-3). In the beginning death enters the world, but in the end death is put to death (Gen. 3:3; 4:6-8; 6:3; Rev. 20:14; 21:4). In the beginning sinful mankind hides from God, but in the end they will look into God's face (Gen. 3:8-11; Rev. 22:4). In the beginning sinful people are banished from God's presence, but in the end God lives among His people within a new heaven and a new earth (Gen. 3:24; Rev. 21:3, 7, 22; 22:4). In the beginning creation deteriorates, but in the end all things are made new (Gen. 5:6, 8, 14, 17, 20, 27, 31; 6:3; Rev. 21:5). Bottom line – in the end, heaven wins (Dan. 4:26; Rev. 19:6)! That is the grand story of the Bible and the main point of Revelation.

In the midst of a world where Christ is a swear word, where Satan is hard at work, where sickness and death plague our everyday lives, and where God's people are despised and persecuted, it is easy to forget that in the end, we win with Jesus. We are on the right side of the argument, and even though we might lose some battles along the way, we will win the war. The book of Revelation was written to comfort the persecuted church of Asia Minor and to remind them that God sees their tears, hears their prayers, assures their victory, and will avenge their blood. Christ, who is the Head of the Church, will have the last word (Rev. 19:15-16). God, who is the Sovereign over all the nations, will have the last laugh (Ps. 2:4). The early Christians needed to be reminded that all is well that ends well, and so do we (Eccles. 7:8)! Remember, we can't lose for winning (2 Cor. 2:14)!

God, Yours is the victory!
Remind me that I am on the winning team.
In Jesus' Name, amen.

Perfect Timing

He has made everything beautiful in its time. Also he has put eternity in their hearts, except that no one can find out the work that God does from beginning to end.

(ECCLESIASTES 3:11)

Phillips Brooks, the former New England clergyman, was known for his calm, cool demeanor. So you can guess the surprise of his associates when they found him pacing up and down the floor of his study like a lion in a cage. One of the friends asked, 'What is the trouble, Dr Brooks?' He abruptly responded, 'The trouble is that I am in a hurry, but God isn't.'

There are times when we feel as if heaven's clock is off by a few days, months, or even years. God seems to be taking His time in answering that prayer, meeting that need, changing that circumstance, or bringing justice. We sit in the waiting room unattended and anxious. We lay awake at night, staring into the darkness with dread. We pace up and down our office in a panic. When we feel upset, guess whose clock needs to be reset?

One of the great paradoxes is that the eternal God is always on time (Eccles. 3:11). He who has sat upon His throne forever and stands beyond the ordered sequence of temporal events nevertheless pays the strictest attention to the march of time. Our times are in His sovereign and secure hands (Ps. 31:15). All our days, and all that fills our days, are written down in His book (Ps. 139:16). The fact is that God's timing is perfect.

Ask Abraham's servant. He was on the road for weeks to search for a bride for Isaac. He happened to arrive at a well at the exact time Isaac's future wife was coming to water her sheep (Gen. 24:14-15). What a coincidence? No, what providence!

Ask the Shunnamite woman. Her son had been brought back to life by the prophet Elisha. Several years later she went to see the king about a property dispute. Lo and behold, Elisha's servant was standing in the king's presence at that very moment recounting the woman's story (2 Kings 8:5). What a coincidence? No, what providence!

Ask Mary and Joseph. They were compelled to return to their place of birth for the purposes of a census under Caesar

Augustus. There in the town of Bethlehem Jesus would be born at the right time and the right place (Gal. 4:4; Micah 5:2; Luke 2:1-6). What a coincidence? No, what providence!

The eternal God is always on time. In all these cases, God orchestrated the details that brought the pieces together at the right time so that His plan would unfold in the right way. God is not in a hurry. He knows what He is doing in us, for us, and around us. God deserves our trust and requires our patience. Don't forget to set your watch to heaven's time!

> *God, thank You that You're always on time.*
> *My trust is a must.*
> *In Jesus' Name, amen.*

You Have the Right to Remain Silent

Lord, my heart is not haughty, Nor my eyes lofty. Neither do I concern myself with great matters, Nor with things too profound for me. Surely I have calmed and quieted my soul, Like a weaned child with his mother; Like a weaned child is my soul within me.

(PSALM 131:1-2)

In 1758, Princeton College called Jonathan Edwards to be their next president. The New England theologian went ahead of his wife, Sarah, to begin the new job. Meanwhile, she stayed back to wrap things up on the home front. In the in-between, Edwards dies tragically through a smallpox inoculation. Sarah receives the news from a courier explaining the tragic facts. They had been married for more than thirty years, and were still deeply in love. Left alone with a brood of children to raise and suffering from rheumatism to such a degree that she could hardly write, she scribbles out this note to her grown daughter Esther: 'What shall I say? A holy and good God has covered us with a black cloud. O that we may kiss the rod, and lay our hands on our mouth! The Lord has done it. He has made me adore His goodness, that we had him [Jonathan] so long. But my God lives; and He has my heart . . . We are all given to God; and there I am, and love to be.'[1]

Sarah Edwards's silence and submission before God in the face of such suffering is a model response we would all do well to emulate. She accepts her trial as from the hand of God and reflexively places her own hand over her mouth to prevent the questioning of God's ways and wisdom (Job 40:4). She finds resolution for her pain, not in understanding, but in faith (Job 13:15; 23:10). She trusts herself and family to the unending love and unerring sovereignty of God. She believed that God was too kind to be cruel, too wise to make a mistake, and too deep to explain Himself.

King David in Psalm 131 models this pattern of saying nothing against God, but rather trusting God implicitly amidst

---

1. W. P. Farley, *Outrageous Mercy* (Grand Rapids, MI: Baker House 2004), p. 168.

life's crosses and losses. In Psalm 131:1, the psalmist admits that he found an inner calm and contentment. He had quieted his soul like a weaned child, by trusting God with those things that were hard to understand. He had stopped trying to make sense of those things that seemed unreasonable and inexplicable! He says: 'Neither do I concern myself with great matters, nor with things too profound for me.' The word 'profound' is the same word that appears in Genesis 18:14 where it is translated 'hard' or 'difficult'. It speaks of things that are God-sized, things beyond our comprehension (Deut. 17:8). We are speaking about things too big and too baffling for us to get our heads around (Ps. 139:6; Job 42:3). While God has made Himself known to us, there are certain things about Him and His dealings with us that are past finding out (Deut. 29:29; Isa. 55:8-9; Rom. 11:33). It is then that we need to follow the examples of Sarah Edwards and King David! We ought not to busy ourselves with problems we cannot solve or questions we cannot answer. We need to give God credit for understanding a few more things than we do. As Spurgeon noted: 'Where we cannot trace the hand of God we need to trust the heart of God' (Ps. 46:10; Isa. 50:10).

God, You are allowed to have Your secrets.
Help me to know that knowing You is enough.
In Jesus' Name, amen.

I Know You

O LORD You have searched me and known me. You know my sitting down and my rising up.

(PSALM 139:1-2)

Amy Carmichael was a young girl from Belfast, my home city, who gave her life to God. She gave her heart to India for fifty years, establishing the now famous Dohnavur Fellowship. Her focus centered on rescuing and reclaiming young girls who were being forced into prostitution to support the priests of the local Hindu temples. Later in life, Amy suffered a horrible fall that confined her to bed. She never returned to Northern Ireland. It is said that from her bed she spent her last days praying, counseling, and witnessing to many. Above her bed she had two plaques. One said, 'Fear Not,' while the other said, 'I know.'

I love it, and I get it! Each and every day Amy Carmichael reminded herself and those who visited her that one need not fear a known present or an unknown future if one understands that God knows all about us, what we are going through, and what it will take to get us through. Our knowledge of His knowledge of us is a great comfort to the anxious heart and affords the believer a place to stand amidst the swirl of changing circumstances. To know that we are known to God and loved by God is all we need to know when the chips are down and the problems of life are piling up. It was a blessing to Job to know that God knows (Job 23:10)! It was an encouragement to David to know that God knows (Ps. 103:14)! And it was a help to the disciples of Jesus to know that God knows (Matt. 6:8)!

The truth that we are never out of God's mind or beyond the reach of His love is wonderfully communicated in Psalm 139, a psalm written by King David. This is a celebratory song that extols the exhaustive knowledge of God and His personal interest in our lives (vv. 17-18). First, God knows us personally (vv. 1-6). God knows us better than we know ourselves. He knows our every movement, action, thought, and word. Second, God knows us physically (vv. 7-16). He knows where we are and who we are. The feet that God made can never take us to a place on earth where God's eyes do not follow. The God who saw us yet unformed in our mother's womb has never lost sight of us for a second. Third, God knows us prophetically (v. 16). God not only knows our past and present but also our future. As one version puts it: 'All of our days have been written down in God's book, and planned before a single one of them began.' The Christian does not need to fear tomorrow, for God is already there.

The big takeaway from Psalm 139 is that in the final analysis the most amazing thing about being a Christian is not that we know God, but that He knows us. And His knowledge of us is the knowledge of a lover. God is not a computer-like figure, crunching the numbers on human life. Rather, He is a God who loves to love us, watching out for our welfare. The Old Testament would remind us that we are graven on the palms of God's hands, and the New Testament would remind us that those hands are nail-scarred (Isa. 49:16; John 20:25). Fear not, for He knows!

God, thank You that You know all things,
and that's all I need to know.
In Jesus' Name, amen.

It's Personal

I am the good shepherd; and I know My sheep, and am known by My own.

(JOHN 10:14)

In the thick of the American Civil War, Senator Charles Sumner, who was consumed by the great idea and ideal of the abolition of slavery, was asked by Julia Ward Howe to meet some friends of hers who had been victims of the scourge of slavery. Julia Ward Howe was the writer of 'The Battle Hymn of the Republic'. To her surprise, he refused and in a condescending manner said, 'Really, Julia, I have lost all interest in individuals.' She answered, 'Why, Charles, God hasn't got as far as that yet!'[2]

Julia Ward Howe was right! Despite the fact that God dwells in heaven, He is sovereign over all living things, and has a plan for the ages, He has not lost interest in the individual. With God it's personal. Jesus, speaking of His love for His people through the metaphor of the shepherd, says: 'I know My sheep' (John 10:14). In fact, He knows them individually by name (John 10:3).

Did you realize the personal nature of the relationship between the Middle Eastern shepherd and his sheep? It is still seen to this day in the shepherd's uncanny ability to divide flocks that have blended at a well or during the night, by simply calling his sheep, whereupon they separate from the other sheep and begin to follow their shepherd. In the Middle East shepherding is personal. There is a closeness between the shepherd and his flock. We know from elsewhere in the Gospels that if a sheep gets lost, the loving shepherd leaves the others in an open field to find it, and when that sheep is rescued, he calls his friends to celebrate the fact that one individual sheep has been returned to the fold (Luke 15:3-7).

Likewise, with God it's personal! His love is tailored, His care is focused, His patience is particular, and His grace is measured to each of us in unique ways. David knew that with God it's personal! He begins his famous twenty-third psalm with 'The

---

2.   G. Avery Lee, *Elijah: Yahweh is My God* (Nashville, TN: Broadman Press, 1987), p. 33.

Lord is *my* Shepherd' (Ps. 23:1). To God, David was not one among many, but one to whom God pays particular attention. David never felt lost amongst the crowd. If, as Martin Luther notes, 'True religion is a matter of personal pronouns,' then this psalm is an outstanding example of that. This psalm is fifty-seven words in the Hebrew Bible and 118 words in the English text of the NKJV. Of note is the fact that 25 percent of the psalm is made up of twenty-eight personal pronouns. David knew that God knew him! David was not just a number to God, but a real name! God knew all about him (Ps. 139:1-6). And that is why Psalm 23 is so universally loved because it is so individual and so personal. Everybody is somebody to God. The personal pronoun 'my' means that all of God is interested in all of me. I can be sure of His time all the time. I can be sure of His love as if I were the only one. I may be part of His flock, but I am a one-of-a-kind sheep to Him.

When Prince Albert died, Queen Victoria sadly said, 'Now there is no one to call me Victoria.' In the midst of life's losses and crosses, it is a blessing to know that God will always call us by our name. He knows us! He knows the way we take (Job 23:10). He knows our frame (Ps. 103:14). He knows our needs (Matt. 6:8). He knows where we dwell (Rev. 2:13). God never loses sight of who we are, what we need, or where we are.

With God it's personal!

God, I praise Your name that You know my name and care
about my life.
In Jesus' Name, amen.

Surviving
the Struggle to Find Peace

In the Know

But you have an anointing from the Holy One, and you know all things.

(1 JOHN 2:20)

A man in New York City had a wife who had a cat. Actually, the cat had her. She loved the cat. She stroked it, combed its fur, fed, and pampered it. The man detested the cat. He was allergic to cat hair. He hated the smell of the litter box. He couldn't stand the scratching on the furniture. And to top it off, he couldn't enjoy a good night's sleep because the cat kept jumping on the bed. When his wife was out of town for the weekend, he put the cat in a bag with some rocks, dumped it in the Hudson River, and uttered a joyful goodbye to the cat. When his wife returned and could not find her cat, she was overwhelmed with grief.

Her husband said, 'Look, honey, I know how much that cat meant to you. I am going to put an ad in the paper and give a reward for five hundred dollars to anyone who finds the cat.' No cat showed up. So a few days later he said, 'Honey, you mean more to me than anything in the world and I want to see you happy again. I will tell you what I will do. I will buy another ad and raise the ante. We will increase the ad to one thousand dollars.' A friend saw the ad and exclaimed, 'You must be nuts! There isn't a cat on earth that is worth a thousand dollars.' The man replied, 'Well, when you know what I know, you can afford to be generous.'[1]

I love that story, and it reminds us that being 'in the know' on something can have a profound effect on a person's attitudes and actions (2 Pet. 3:17). When you think about it, the Christian uniquely is a person in the know (1 John 2:20)! '*We know* that we have passed from death to life because we love the brethren' (1 John 3:14). '*We know* that all things work together for good to them that love God' (Rom. 8:28). '*We know* that if our earthly house, this tent, is destroyed, we have a building from God, a house not made with hands, eternal in the heavens' (2 Cor. 5:1).

---

1. Haddon Robinson, *What Jesus Said About Successful Living* (Grand Rapids, MI: Discovery House Publishers, 1991), p. 213.

'*We know* that when Christ shall appear we shall be like Him' (1 John 3:1). '*We know* that the Son of God has come and given us understanding and *we know* Him who is true' (1 John 5:20). '*We know* Him who said "Vengeance is mine"' (Heb. 10:30). '*We know* that Christ hears us, whatever we ask' (1 John 5:15).

That is just a smattering of what the Christian knows, and knowing it should affect the way we think and act. Like the man in our story, when you know what we know, you can afford quite a few things. You can afford to have a confidence about your salvation. You can afford to believe that good can come from bad. You can afford to pray audaciously. You can afford to leave justice with God. And you can afford to grow old gracefully knowing that the best is yet to come. Do others know that what you know has changed your life?

God, the greatest thing I know is You Yourself.
Help me to live out the radical realities of what I know.
In Jesus' Name, amen.

Sleep Well

There are many who say, 'Who will show us any good?'
LORD, lift up the light of Your countenance upon us. You
have put gladness in my heart, More than in the season
that their grain and wine increased. I will both lie down in
peace, and sleep; For You alone, O LORD, make me dwell
in safety.

(PSALM 4:6-8)

The news of Japan's surprise attack upon the American fleet at
Pearl Harbor on December 7, 1941 was a bittersweet affair to the
British wartime leader Sir Winston Churchill. It was bitter in the
sense that he mourned the great loss of ships and sailors in this
unprovoked attack. But it was sweet in the sense that it would
become the catalyst for America's entry into the Second World
War. The sleeping giant had been awakened, and surely now the
tide would turn against Germany. The country of his mother's
birth would now be arrayed on Britain's side. It is reported that
on the evening of that infamous day Churchill said, 'Tonight
I shall sleep the sleep of the saved and thankful!'

'The sleep of the saved' – now there is an interesting and
intriguing phrase! By inference, Churchill's words assume that
those who know God and are known to God sleep better than
most, or at least they ought to. Their rest is not found in downy
pillows or soft pillow top mattresses, but in God who can be
trusted with all their cares and concerns (Ps. 55:22; 1 Pet. 5:7).

King David is a case in point. He writes in the fourth Psalm:
'In peace I will lie down and sleep; for you alone, O Lord, make
me dwell in safety' (Ps. 4:8). The backdrop to this psalm is
Absalom's rebellion, which makes these words stand out even
more (2 Sam. 15–18). David is at rest amidst unrest. David is at
peace amidst war. How was he able to sleep at all? According to
Psalm 4 because of God's smile (v. 6), God's sufficiency (v. 7), and
God's security (v. 8)! True calm and contentment depends, not
on circumstances, but on God's loving kindness and promised
faithfulness. David was able to sleep in the presence of his
enemies, just as Jesus was able to sleep in the midst of a storm
(Ps. 23:5; Mark 4:38-9).

Statistics show that seventy million Americans have trouble sleeping. Thirty tons of aspirins, sleeping pills, and tranquilizers are consumed every day. America is up when she should be down. When the anxieties of the day are robbing you of a good night's slumber, pray to God for the gift of sleep and ask your Father in heaven to tuck you in with the sure and certain knowledge that in the morning you will find new mercies for the coming day (Pss. 127:2; 3:5; Lam. 3:22-3)!

Let God work the nightshift (Ps. 121:4). You can rest and sleep, for God is at work on your behalf (Eph. 1:11). Even though at times it might seem as if God is sleeping or snoring, it is never the case. Read Esther chapter six and learn how God turns the tables on Mordecai's enemy Haman, even as Mordecai sleeps (Esther 6:1-13). Ironically, Haman will be hanged on the very gallows he had built for Mordecai (Esther 7:10). Listen and learn! God's got your back, so you go ahead and lie on yours, and sleep the sleep of the saved.

God, thank You that You're always awake.
Help that reality be the lullaby that puts me to sleep.
In Jesus' Name, amen.

Don't Worry About a Thing

*But seek first the kingdom of God and His righteousness,
and all these things shall be added to you. Therefore do not
worry about tomorrow, for tomorrow will worry about its
own things. Sufficient for the day is its own trouble.*

(MATTHEW 6:33-4)

A lady visited the doctor and told him that she was feeling
rather run down. As far as she could tell, her get up and go had
got up and gone. After examining his patient, the doctor replied,
'Madam, it is my expert opinion that you are not all run down,
but you are all wound up.'

That diagnosis describes a lot of people today, wound up
in knots of anxiety and apprehension. They are worried about
losing their house to the bank, their job to overseas, their sons
to war, their spouse to another, their freedoms to a judge, their
life to cancer, and even their salvation to sin. Some people are
worried about the fact that they are not worried. While we
wrestle with worry, Jesus in the Sermon on the Mount challenges
us to come to grips with it and to flat out stop it (Matt. 6:25, 34).
He commands us to cease and desist! The Lord Jesus sees worry,
not primarily as an illness that needs to be treated, but as a sin
that needs to be repented of and stopped.

Here are a few reasons why:

Worry is *fruitless* (Matt. 6:27). Worry is a futile exercise in
that it doesn't add a single hour to anyone's life. It is a lot of
work for nothing. In fact, it makes things worse rather than
better, in that it makes us unfit to deal with the situation that
has us so uptight in the first place. It distracts our ability to
focus and leaves us feeling tired and tense. Worry doesn't
change a thing except the person who is worrying, and not for
the good. Someone has rightly said, 'Worry is like a rocking
chair. It gives you something to do, but it doesn't get you
anywhere.'

Worry is *faithless* (Matt. 6:30). The worrier is someone
whose faith is small. According to Jesus, the disciples were
deficient in their trust towards God. They were not reflecting

on God's past and promised faithfulness. They lacked faith in the faithfulness of God, and that which is not of faith is sin (Rom. 14:23; Heb. 11:6). Anxiety, then, is not only a waste of emotional energy; it is an expression of spiritual forgetfulness and faithlessness. Anxiety envisages circumstances that may never occur or cannot be changed, while forgetting truths about God's unchanging character and care.

Worry is *fatherless* (Matt. 6:31-2). Jesus understands that an orphaned world without God and hope scurries around in fits of anxiety, speculating about stuff. What He doesn't understand is the anxiety of those whom God has adopted into His family by grace. Children from caring homes with good fathers don't worry, and neither should those belonging to God's family. Worry is practical atheism, as well as an affront to our Father in heaven. Worry is no respectable sin. It is *fruitless, faithless,* and *fatherless.*

> *God, You are my faithful Father.*
> *Forgive me for living as though I'm forgotten*
> *rather than favored.*
> *In Jesus' Name, amen.*

Running Gets You Nowhere

Give ear to my prayer, O God, and do not hide Yourself from my supplication.

(PSALM 55:1)

There are times in life when things can get so bad that running away seems like the best and only solution. That is why each and every day people quit their jobs, file for divorce, leave the ministry, or drop out of school. They have run out of steam and so they run. They envy the very birds that are flying overhead and wish that they too could migrate to another warmer and sunnier place.

In Psalm 55, King David envies the birds above his head. His life situation is so painful that he wishes he had the wings of a dove to fly away and find some peace and quiet (Ps. 55:6-8; cp. Jer. 9:2-6). The fifty-fifth psalm chronicles a bewildering and bitter episode in King David's life when his friends had become his enemies. David had been stabbed in the back by someone who had pretended to be on his side but later became the leader of his opposition (Ps. 55:13-14, 20-21). The setting is unknown, but it may relate to his son Absalom's rebellion (2 Sam. 18–19) or his friend's Ahithophel's conspiracy (2 Sam. 15:31, 34).

Ultimately, the key to handling this situation for David was not found in running away from the problem, but in running to the Lord with the problem (Ps. 55:22). It was an escape of sorts, but it was an escape into the presence of God where sustaining grace was to be found. It is in the Lord's presence by means of worship and prayer that we exchange the wings of a dove for the wings of an eagle (Ps. 55:6; Isa. 40:31). A dove will fly ahead of the storm, but an eagle will fly above the storm.

There is an alternative to running from life, and it is the strengthening presence of God enabling us to stand up to life. There is sustaining grace. The Lord does not promise to save us *from* the burdens of life, but to sustain us *in* them. The Lord didn't save the three Hebrew children *from* the fiery furnace; He saved them *in* the fiery furnace. Jesus prayed in the garden at Gethsemane that the bitter cup of the cross might pass from Him. It did not, but God sustained Christ in the garden, on the cross, and brought him through the valley of the shadow of death victoriously.

In the summer of 1940, 338,000 British and Allied troops were rescued from the beaches of Dunkirk, France in what can only be described as a miracle of deliverance. Winston Churchill, however, sought to temper the euphoric mood of the British people with these words: 'Wars are not won by evacuations.' It must be added, neither is life.

Therefore don't be praying for tasks equal to your strength; pray for grace equal to your tasks. We don't have to run in fear when we walk with God in faith (Isa. 43:2).

God, thank You for Your sustaining grace in the trials of life.
I ask for Your grace to fly like an eagle instead of a dove.
In Jesus' Name, amen.

Look Who's Talking

Why are you cast down, O my soul? And why are you disquieted within me? Hope in God, for I shall yet praise Him for the help of His countenance.

(Psalm 42:5)

During my time as a police officer in Northern Ireland, we were shown a training video that advocated the importance of speaking positively to oneself should you be shot or seriously injured in the line of duty. Speaking calmly, consistently, and confidently to oneself about a positive outcome was said to help the injured officer from going into shock. It was not a guarantee of survival, but it helped an officer give himself a fighting chance. Studies from several police departments in the USA show that certain officers had died from gunshot wounds that seemed survivable. Medical examiners and investigators concluded that the police officers had probably said to themselves, 'I am shot and I am going to die.' They did not help themselves by what they said to themselves. Their words became a self-fulfilling prophecy. The message of the video to us that day was that what we say to ourselves is vastly important.

In Psalm 42, we meet a Levite in a rather melancholic mood (vv. 5, 11). This son of Korah is at low tide physically, emotionally, and spiritually (vv. 3, 7, 9). He is cast down in spirit due to the fact that he is living in exile from the Temple in Jerusalem, possibly in Aram, Assyria, or Babylon (vv. 1-2, 4). To make matters worse, his enemies taunt him on a daily basis regarding the seeming lack of God's presence and protection in his life (vv. 3, 10). Here is a man who is physically alive, but dying on the inside, a man adrift on a sea of wild emotions. The author of this ancient poem is a man bent over with care, dealing with the absence of desirable things and the presence of difficult things. Can you relate?

Of interest to us is the fact that the psalmist looks his depression square in the eye and faces up to his feelings. He does not allow himself the luxury of self-pity. Therefore, the writer begins to interrogate, interrupt, and instruct himself. 'Why are you cast down, O my soul,' he asks himself (vv. 5, 11). He talks to himself; he does not allow self to talk to him. He takes charge of the conversation that has been raging in his head. He begins to steer his internal thoughts in a more godly direction. Like this psalm, other psalms are full of self-talk, reminding us of the need to actively and aggressively talk sense and Scripture to ourselves (Pss 62:5; 103:1-5). Ordering our thoughts away from the bad and unto the good, away from lies and unto truth, and away from self and unto God is the path to peace (Phil. 4:6-9).

Listen to Ben Patterson as he writes about this psalm, and this issue: 'Feelings can be like unruly children, and like unruly children they must not be allowed to have the last word. Let them sound off, but then tell yourself what is true ... Talk back to yourself and affirm the truth that "I will praise Him again – my Savior and my God."'[2]

Remember! Talking to yourself is not a sign of insanity.

> *God, I pay tribute to Your truthfulness.*
> *Help me to talk truth to myself today.*
> *In Jesus' Name, amen.*

---

2.   Ben Patterson, *God's Prayer Book* (Coral Stream, IL: Saltriver, 2008), p. 126.

It Comes with a Guarantee

Now He who establishes us with you in Christ and has anointed us is God, who also has sealed us and given us the Spirit in our hearts as a guarantee.

(2 CORINTHIANS 1:21-2)

When a young couple get married, they immediately dream of getting their own house. They work hard and set about saving their money for a down payment on their dream house. Finally the day arrives when they draw up the papers to buy the house. They meet with the bank officials, sign the documents, and hand them a check for the down payment. The down payment does not represent the full price of the house. It's only a portion, but it is the promise of more payments to come. Often thirty years of payments until the full price is paid.

With that picture in mind, we would do well to remind ourselves that the Holy Spirit has been given to those who trust in Christ as God's down payment regarding the promise of eternal life. In his second letter to the Corinthians, Paul tells them that, upon believing in Christ, God has 'given us the Spirit in our hearts as a guarantee' (2 Cor. 1:22). The word 'guarantee' carries the idea of a pledge or deposit, guaranteeing that the full amount will be paid. Therefore, in the gift of the Holy Spirit at salvation, God is in effect guaranteeing the Christian's complete redemption (Phil. 1:6). God is promising our full and final inheritance of eternal life at the coming of Christ (Eph. 1:13-14 ; 4:30). The further payments promised in this pledge represent nothing less than the realities and glories of heaven for every child of God.

On the one hand, the down payment of the Holy Spirit breeds assurance. Here is a promise of the full redemption of body, soul, and spirit (Eph. 1:13-14; 4:30). The Holy Spirit indwelling and sealing the believer is God's 'earnest money', pledged against our full redemption and glorification in Christ. That is remarkable and reassuring! God our Father has made Himself the guarantee of our salvation and God is not about to default on His promises. The fact and implication is that if God does not keep the pledge, He would cease to be God, but God cannot deny Himself

(2 Tim. 2:13). He is faithful and will do it (1 Thess. 5:23-4). The security of the believer is as sure as God is true. What a relief!

On the other hand, the down payment of the Holy Spirit breeds anticipation. Remember, the guarantee is the promise of something more. The gift of the Holy Spirit is the first installment of all that God is going to do for us (1 Cor. 2:9-10). In Christ we go from glory to glory (Prov. 4:18; 2 Cor. 3:18). Salvation is moving toward an intended end and God's love for us grows wider and deeper each and every day. None of us are what we shall be in God's presence someday (1 John 3:1-3). The gift of the Holy Spirit is a reminder that the Christian has everything to live and die for. The best is yet to come! The gift of the Spirit is like being allowed into the kitchen to have a little taste of the feast to come.

God, thank You that my future is bright.
Help me to live now in the assurance and anticipation
of a future 100 per cent guaranteed by You.
In Jesus' Name, amen.

Safe and Sound

Blessed be the God and Father of our Lord Jesus Christ, who according to His abundant mercy has begotten us again to a living hope through the resurrection of Jesus Christ from the dead, to an inheritance incorruptible and undefiled and that does not fade away, reserved in heaven for you, who are kept by the power of God through faith for salvation ready to be revealed in the last time.

(1 PETER 1:3-5)

In his book *Muscular Faith*, author and campus pastor Ben Patterson writes:

> When circumstances aren't as agreeable as I want them to be, I practice a little spiritual discipline that has managed to feed my hope and keep me in joy, nevertheless. I have a long version and a short version: Someone will ask me how I am, and I'll answer, 'Other than the fact that all my sins are forgiven, and that I am going to live in heaven eternally in the joy of God, I am not doing too well.' The look on the questioner's face always amuses me. That and the irony of saying I am not doing too well in the face of such magnificent prospects, usually lifts the cloud a bit. That is the long version. The short version is simply to answer, 'I am fundamentally sound.' I may be superficially bummed out, sad, frustrated, angry, but that is the worst I can say about it; it is surface only.[3]

Fundamentally sound is indeed a great way to describe the Christian's condition. The Christian may experience loss, change, upset, or setback, but when you scratch beneath the surface, things are fundamentally sound. Whatever life takes or time steals, it does not rob us of our spiritual blessings in Christ. Essentially, the Christian's life is unassailable.

In the opening of Peter's first letter, the apostle begins with a recital of the blessings enjoyed by God's redeemed children (1 Pet. 1:3-5). Peter reminds his readers living in this temporary

---

3. Ben Patterson, *Muscular Faith* (Coral Stream, IL: Saltriver, 2011), p. 176.

and troubled world that through the death and resurrection of Christ, God has brought them to a state of new birth. The result of being born again is that they have acquired an eternal inheritance reserved in heaven. It is an inheritance in Christ that can never perish, spoil, or fade. What the saint of God has in Christ is something that remains untouched by decay, unstained by evil, and unimpaired by time. Through faith in Christ, the Christian has been granted a brand new life and has everything to live for, including a bright future in heaven!

Life may pilfer from us friends and family, health and wealth, but that which is most essential and wonderful remains unsoiled and unspoiled. The implication of Peter's words is that you and I have a guaranteed future in Christ. We have a spiritual trust fund that no one can touch. All the things that are really worth living for and dying with are locked safely away in heaven's vault. No one can separate us from the love of God (Rom. 8:38-9). Nothing can rob us of His forgiveness (1 John 1:9; Micah 7:19). No one can take His Holy Spirit from us (Eph. 1:13). Nothing can reverse our deliverance from the penalty, power, and presence of sin (Col. 1:13; Rom. 6:14; Ps. 103:12; Rev. 22:3). No one can tamper with our justification and adoption (Titus 3:7).[4] Our relationship with God and our riches in God are never at risk.

Safe and sound is a good description of a Christian's life and lot!

God, You are a steady source and formidable force. Whether
I feel up or down, help me know that I am safe and sound.
In Jesus' Name, amen.

---

4. Adapted from *Lost in the Middle* by Paul David Tripp (Wapwallopen, PA: Shepherd Press, 2004), p. 195.

Dead Calm

*Then He arose and rebuked the wind, and said to the sea,
'Peace, be still!' And the wind ceased and there was a great
calm. But He said to them, 'Why are you so fearful? How is
it that you have no faith?' And they feared exceedingly, and
said to one another, 'Who can this be, that even the wind
and the sea obey Him!'*

(MARK 4:39-41)

There is a likable story that comes from a naval academy in
England. On a particular day, a top officer in the British Navy
visited the depot and began barking questions at the students
to determine their preparedness for the rigors of commanding
a ship at sea. Cornering one student, the admiral asked, 'What
would you do if a storm blew up?' The student snapped back,
'Lower the anchor, sir!' The admiral retorted, 'What would
you do if the anchor broke away and another storm blew up?'
Without skipping a beat the student replied, 'Lower another
anchor, sir!' Pressing his case the admiral asked, 'What would
you do if that anchor broke away and a third storm blew up!'
Sticking to his guns the student answered, 'Lower another
anchor, sir!' More than a little frustrated the commanding
officer snorted, 'And where are you getting all these anchors?'
The student replied, 'Same place that you are getting all the
storms from, sir!'[5]

Those storms may have been imagined, but the point being
made by the admiral was very real. Every British naval officer
needs to know how to navigate his way through a heaving sea.
And what is true of life in the navy is true of life itself! We all
need to know how to deal with sudden storms and squalls that
blow up in our face. Storms can be death, illness, demonic
attacks, besetting sins, loss of income, divorce, crime, church
conflict, and perhaps a suffocating sense of defeat. Interestingly,
saints of old have likened their trials and troubles to sudden
storms (Pss. 18:16; 69:1-3; 144:7).

---

5. Phil Moore, *Galatians to Colossians* (Oxford, UK: Monarch Books,
    2014), p. 217.

To help us chart a path through life's storms, let's briefly examine several principles that emerge out of the story of Jesus calming the storm (Mark 4:35-41):

First, peace is found in knowing that even in the midst of a storm, God intends for you to be there. One of the striking features about this story is that they undertook this journey at Christ's command (v. 35). They were not out of the will of God, but following it. There was a divine intentionality in this storm encounter. Jesus willed it. He purposed it, and He had purposes in it.

Second, peace is found in fighting the temptation to doubt God's love in the face of God's apparent disinterest or distance. The disciples wrongly questioned Christ's care of them (vv. 38-40). Jesus' sleep was intended to awaken in them a greater trust, but they failed because of fear.

Third, peace is found in focusing on the glory and power of Christ (v. 41). Their fear of the storm was replaced by a greater fear of the One who had calmed the storm. There stood in their midst the creator of all living things. Peace doesn't come from finding calmer waters, but from having Jesus in the boat.

Remember, what Jesus did physically in stilling the wind and the waves, He can do emotionally and spiritually for you. Jesus can bring peace to the troubled mind and quiet to the restless soul (Isa. 26:3). His miracles are meant to point to a greater spiritual reality (Mark 2:9-12). They move from the lesser to the greater, from the physical to the spiritual. So in the storms of life, the believer finds an anchor in the inexplicable peace that comes through trusting Christ (John 14:27; Phil. 4:6-7). With Christ in the vessel you can smile at the storm!

God, thank You that Your presence is the promise of peace.
Make me to keep calm and carry on.
In Jesus' Name, amen.

Surviving
the Struggle to Worship and Give Thanks

Don't Forget to Say 'Thank You'

*It is good to give thanks to the LORD, and to sing praises to
Your name, O Most High.*

(PSALM 92:1)

One Sunday morning following the service, a woman came up
to the pastor and thanked him for the encouraging and edifying
sermon he had just preached. He replied, 'Thank you, but don't
thank me, thank the Lord.' She said, 'Well, I thought of that, but
it wasn't quite that good.'

It is a sad thing when God's people cannot quite bring
themselves to give thanks to the Lord. What a pity that in
a world so full of God's goodness and mercy that it should be so
empty of His praise. The Bible would remind us that it is a good
thing to give thanks to the Lord (Pss. 92:1; 118:29). Here are some
good things for which to be thankful:

Things (1 Tim. 6:17): Things are not all important in life, but
they are important. All of us, especially we Americans, have
lots of things for which we should be grateful. Our homes
and garages are an Aladdin's Cave of stuff.

Health (Ps. 103:3-4): Health and strength are among life's
most precious gifts. To be able bodied, and in use of our
facilities is a matter of great thankfulness. We need to be on
our knees in thanks that we are on our feet at all.

Adversity (Rom. 5:3-4): Adversity is God's sandpaper to rub
off the rough edges of our character and make us more like
Christ. We can thank God for our trials, for there is purpose
to our pain. We come to know Him in fuller dimensions as
a result of hurt and hassle. Travels broaden us, but troubles
deepen us.

Now (Ps. 118:24): There is no time like the present. The reason
so many people find it hard to be happy is that they view the
past as better than it was and the future as better than it will
be. Today is all we need, all we can handle, and all we have.

Kindness (Phil. 4:10-16): The care of others for us is an
extreme blessing. No man is an island, and our lives are

greatly enriched by the daily deposits of kind friends, family and strangers.

Salvation (Col. 1:12-13): The greatest gift of all is eternal life through our Lord Jesus Christ. There is no greater wealth than the riches of His grace. There is no greater health than soundness of soul.

Remember, it is a good thing to give thanks to the Lord!

> *God, thank You for all these things and many more.*
> *You are the Giver and the ultimate gift.*
> *In Jesus' Name, amen.*

Updating Our Worship

And when I saw Him, I fell at His feet as dead. But He laid His right hand on me, saying to me, 'Do not be afraid; I am the First and the Last. I am He who lives, and was dead, and behold, I am alive forevermore. Amen. And I have the keys of Hades and of Death.'

(REVELATION 1:17-18)

The worship offered to God in most churches on Sunday needs updating. It needs to become more contemporary, but not in the way most people think. When I talk about the need for more contemporary worship in our churches, I am not thinking in terms of bands versus orchestras, or worship teams versus choir, or even throwing out the hymnal. The update has to do with who we worship, not how we worship.

In a recent study of the book of the Revelation, I was confronted afresh by the thought that this is a book about Jesus. It is the revelation of Jesus Christ, which God gave to the apostle John (Rev. 1:1). It is an unveiling of the once crucified, now risen, and gloried Son of God. It is a divine disclosing of Jesus Christ in His present splendor (Rev. 1–3) and future glory (Rev. 4–22). The stated purpose of this book is to help us see Christ as we have rarely seen Him before (Matt. 17:1-8), not as the lowly carpenter but as the lofty king (Rev. 1:12-18; 19:11-16). He who was crowned with thorns on earth is now crowned with honor in heaven (Phil. 2:9-11). Without this view, the apostle John happily puts his head on the chest of Jesus at the Last Supper (John 13:23). With this view of the post-ascension glory of the Lord Jesus, John falls as a dead man at Christ's feet (Rev. 1:17). John's vision of Jesus had been updated and his worship along with it.

John's prostration alerts us to the danger that unless we update our view of Christ according to the book of the Revelation, we may be committing idolatry in the very act of worship. Our worship of Christ must be contemporary. It must reflect Him as He now is. His humiliation is over. His glory has been restored (John 17:1-5). The world that laughed at Him will soon wail because of Him (Rev. 1:7). He who came the first time to a crucifixion is coming again to a coronation (Rev. 11:15).

Revelation prevents us from committing the sin of idolatry, from worshipping Jesus as someone less than He is.

Whether a church is one hundred years old or one year old, it needs to update its worship in accordance with the book of Revelation. We need to regain our fear of God and lose our familiarity with God. We need to see Jesus sitting on a throne, not hanging on a tree. We need invigorating worship that at the same time scares us half to death just like John.

Upon reaching the summit of a high mountain, a climber braved the cross winds and jumped to his feet in joy. As he did so, an expired guide pulled him down, and said, 'On your knees! You are never safe except on your knees!' As we ascend the holy hill to worship God, we need to do so with a due respect and reverence. Don't forget to download the new worship app from the book of Revelation.

God, I bow down because You are raised up on high!
In Jesus' Name, amen.

Sing Along

And I heard, as it were, the voice of a great multitude, as the sound of many waters and as the sound of mighty thunderings, saying, 'Alleluia! For the Lord God Omnipotent reigns!'

(REVELATION 19:6)

The book of Revelation is a very noisy book. It resounds to the clatter of the thunderbolts of God's just wrath poured out upon a wayward world. From start to finish, it echoes with the sound of war, earthquakes, and demonic beasts. Yet for all its blood and thunder, it is essentially a songbook. Amidst the din of a world at war with itself and God, there are songs to be heard of praise offered up to God by angelic choirs and redeemed souls.

It is an often-overlooked fact that the worship of God forms the background music to the book of the Revelation. There is the anthem of the triune God (Rev. 4:8). There is the creation hymn (4:11). There is the new song of redemption (5:9-10). There is the angel's chorale (5:12-14). There is the martyr's canticle (6:10). There is the kingdom carol (11:15). There is the judgment psalm (11:17-18). There is the shout of the overcomers (12:10-12). There is the song of Moses and the Lamb (15:3-4). And there is the hallelujah chorus (19:1-4, 6).

Beginning in chapter 4 and continuing intermittently through to chapter 19, we have a series of songs around the throne of God that highlight the unchanging reality of an eternal world in which God's purpose is unfailing and in which Christ reigns supreme. History will close and crest with a hallelujah chorus celebrating God's victory over sin and Satan (Rev. 19:6). In the book of Revelation, one throne reigns supreme, and that is God's throne (Rev. 4:2, 10-11; 5:13; 7:9-10; 11:15-18; 19:1-4). Time will tell at the end that all the great figures of history have been minor actors in a major drama written and produced by our Sovereign God and His Son, Jesus Christ (Phil. 2:9-11).

Amidst a troubled and tumbling world, John fixes our gaze upon a throne that stands in heaven, a throne that has been established forever (Rev. 4:2; Ps. 45:6). The book of Revelation therefore reminds us that God has not abdicated His throne. It is true of life that there is much that runs contrary to God's will, but where God does not rule, He overrules. So no matter how dark the day, the Christian can meet it with a song that says: 'Alleluia! For the Lord God Omnipotent reigns!'(Rev. 19:6). The worship we see offered before the throne of God in the book of Revelation is a summons to the Christian to live a joyful life of settled peace in the knowledge that God is in control. In the end, God wins.

While parts of the book of the Revelation are rather dark and stormy, we must not miss the rainbow of a Sovereign God who is worthy of our worship both now and forever (Rev. 4:3).

When my father-in-law came to Christ in his native Scotland, his workmates mocked him by saying, 'Gordon has become a hallelujah.' Well, that is fitting! Every Christian is and ought to be a living hallelujah to our loving and Sovereign God! Today, you sing harmony and I'll sing bass.

God, You deserve full praise!
Help me join in the continuous choir!
In Jesus' Name, amen.

Amazing Grace

And of His fullness we have all received, and grace for grace.

(JOHN 1:16)

In the book *Holy,Holy,Holy*, R. C. Sproul tells the story of his second year in teaching. He had been assigned to teach a class on Old Testament Introduction to 250 college freshmen. As part of the coursework, Dr Sproul required three small papers due on the 30th of September, October, and November. Twenty-five students missed the deadline in September, but he showed some leniency. Next month, some fifty students missed the deadline, and he graciously gave them three more days to turn in their papers. By this stage, Dr Sproul was one of the most popular professors on campus. When November came around, 150 students crossed the deadline, and R.C. started handing out failing grades. One student called Fitzgerald cried foul and protested that what the professor was doing was not fair. Sproul reminded him if it was justice he sought, he could give him an 'F' for his tardiness in October as well. Reflecting on the whole semester, R. C. Sproul said this: 'These students had grown accustomed to my grace. In September they were amazed by grace. In October they were surprised by grace. But by November they were demanding grace. They had forgotten that grace is not an inalienable right or an entitlement you deserve.'[1]

How easy is it for us as Christians to take God's grace for granted, to move from being amazed by it to being accustomed to it. We mistakenly assume upon God's goodness and presume upon His mercy as if it is owed to us. But grace by its very nature is amazing, and it must always be seen as such. Grace is God's *unmerited* favor coming to us despite our sin through Christ. Grace is God's riches at Christ's expense. It is not owed, nor merited. Rather it is granted sovereignly and surprisingly by the indiscriminate love of God. By nature we are hell-deserving sinners, and by grace we are heaven born and heaven bound.

---

1. R. C. Sproul, *Holy, Holy, Holy: Proclaiming the Perfections of God* (Lake Mary, FL: Reformation Trust, 2010), p. 143.

Life, and all its attendant blessings, is an amazing gift from God, and eternal life with its endless joy an even greater gift! According to the apostle John, we have through Christ received from God 'grace upon grace', grace replacing grace (John 1:16). You and I live under the showerhead of God's overflowing grace. On a day to day basis, we are showered with saving grace, strengthening grace, serving grace, singing grace, and sufficient grace (Eph. 2:8-9; 2 Tim. 2:1; Rom. 12:3-8; Col. 3:16; 2 Cor. 12:9). Any good that comes to us, any good in us, any good done by us, is God's good work in Christ. Paul acknowledges he was what he was by the grace of God (1 Cor. 15:10). As an old Scottish saint prayed, 'May God grant us grace to feel our need of grace, then give us grace to ask for grace, then give us grace to receive grace, then when grace has been given, give us grace to be grateful.'

Today, put amazing back into grace!

God, You are a kind King!
Help me to get a grip on grace.
In Jesus' Name, amen.

Count Your Blessings

Bless the LORD, O my soul, and forget not all His benefits
(PSALM 103:2)

The guy was obviously down in the mouth as he sat on the park bench. He was so miserable-looking that a policeman who was patrolling the area sat down and sought to console him. 'Something the matter?' asked the policeman of the young man who was staring into space. 'Yeah,' he said, 'You just wouldn't believe it. Two months ago my grandfather died, and left me $85,000 and some oil wells.' The policeman raised his eyebrows and responded, 'That doesn't sound like something to get upset about.' 'Yeah, but you haven't heard the full story yet. Last month my uncle died and left me $150,000.' The policeman shook his head in bewilderment. 'I don't understand,' he said. 'Why are you sitting here looking so unhappy?' The guy responded, 'So far, this month, not a cent.'[2]

Some people are like that. They think the world owes them a living, or that God owes them a favor. They never seem to be happy with what they have. They never seem to be content. They write their blessings in the sand and engrave their grievances in cement. They tend to forget the bad times during the good times, and in doing so, they overlook God's past faithfulness (Deut. 8:11-14). They tend to forget the good times during the bad times, and in doing so, they charge God with not caring (Job 2:10). They spend little time looking for the silver lining in the cloud. They spend little time savoring the small and steady blessings of life. They spend little time remembering what they have forgotten about – God's goodness and mercy across their lives. They spend little time evaluating the worth of their soul to God and the preciousness of their blood-bought salvation. They never have enough because they spend their days looking at what they do not have and overlooking what they do have.

Psalm 103 acts as a counterbalance to such ingratitude and forgetfulness. In this psalm, David, by example and exhortation,

---

2. Brian Harbour, *Rising Above the Crowd* (Nashville, TN: Broadman Press, 1988), p. 118.

calls us to 'count our blessings and name them one by one, so that we might be surprised afresh at what the Lord has done,' as the old hymn says. David wants to be an instrument of praise with all the stops pulled out (vv. 1, 22). To that end, he cultivates a spirit of thanksgiving through intentional reflection (v. 2). Thinking and thanking go hand in hand. Memory is a handmaiden to worship. In this psalm, David encourages himself and us to do three things:

First, we are to think about what God has given us – salvation, health, protection, and many good things (vv. 1-5)! Second, we are to think about what God has not given us (vv. 8-12). He has not dealt with us according to our sins. Third, we are to think about what God is still to give us (v. 17; Ps. 73:23-4). God's mercy is everlasting and will carry us through the very gates of heaven. Be thankful for what God has given you, and not given you!

God, thank You for not giving me what I do deserve and giving me what I don't deserve.
Help me to count Your innumerable blessings.
In Jesus' Name, amen.

An Attitude of Gratitude

And Jesus took the loaves, and when He had given thanks He distributed them to the disciples, and the disciples to those sitting down; and likewise of the fish, as much as they wanted.

(JOHN 6:11)

G. K. Chesterton was a remarkable individual who belonged to the early twentieth century. His genius combined the abilities of a novelist, critic, poet, popular theologian, and writer of detective stories. Toward the end of his life in 1936, he turned his attention and considerable ability to the writing of his autobiography. As part of the process, he tried to distill into a single sentence the most important lesson he had learned from life. After many false starts and wrong answers, he finally settled on this: 'The chief idea of my life . . . is the idea of taking things with gratitude, and not taking things for granted.' He added elsewhere in the book: 'The aim of life is appreciation: there is no sense in not appreciating things; and there is no sense in having more of them if you have less appreciation of them.'

An attitude of gratitude is indeed a noble and necessary thing. The Bible tells us that it is a good thing to give thanks to the Lord (Ps. 92:1-2). Given the depth of God's love, the breadth of God's mercy, and the height of God's faithfulness to each of us, each of us needs to do a better job at cultivating an attitude of gratitude. God, as the psalmist notes, loads us down with blessings on a daily basis, and therefore the aim of our lives ought to be greater appreciation (Pss 68:19; 103:1-5; 145:2).

To help us cultivate an attitude of gratitude, I thought about the fact that we ought to give thanks to the Lord for the things the Lord gave thanks for. In a recent study, I was struck by the thankfulness of Jesus

First, Jesus gave thanks for food. In John 6:11, Jesus gave thanks for the loaves and fish from which He would feed the five thousand. Christ, the bread of life, paused to thank God for a loaf of bread. In a land of abundant food, like America, may we give thanks to God for our food, the appetite to enjoy it, and the taste buds to savor it (Ps. 103:5)!

Second, Jesus gave thanks for answered prayer. In John 11:41, Jesus thanks the Father for answering His prayer regarding the raising of Lazarus. Surely, we can thank God for the many answers to prayer that litter our path through life. We rejoice that God hears and answers our prayers before we pray (Isa. 65:24), while we pray (Acts 12:1-17), and after we pray (1 Sam. 1:19, 27).

Third, Jesus gives thanks for the fruit of suffering. In Luke 22:19, Jesus gives thanks to the Father for what He was going to accomplish through Christ's death on the cross. Through the brokenness of Jesus, many would be made whole (Isa. 53:5). Christ's suffering would be painful, but clearly profitable. We too, can thank God for the blessed benefits of our trials and tears. Suffering clarifies our values (James 1:2-4, 9-10), makes us more compassionate (2 Cor. 1:4), crushes our pride (2 Cor. 12:1-10), and develops fortitude in us (Rom. 5:1-3).

Like Jesus, let us take things with gratitude, not for granted.

God, thank You for Jesus' example of prayer.
May I look to You with thanks rather than overlook You
without thanks.
In Jesus' Name, amen.

Surviving
the Struggle to Live with
Certain People

Keeping Score

Love ... does not behave rudely, does not seek its own, is not provoked, thinks no evil

(1 CORINTHIANS 13:5)

Recently I read a beautiful story about a grandmother celebrating her fiftieth wedding anniversary. Surrounded by friends and family, she was asked, 'What is the secret of your long marriage?' 'Oh, it is very simple,' she said. 'Before Henry and I got married, I was determined to write down a list of ten things that I would always forgive him quickly for and then forget about. After we got married, Henry would do certain things and I would think, Lucky for him – that one is on the list.' The young wives in the room scrambled to find pens and paper, anxious to copy down the ten items on the old woman's list. 'So tell us, Grandma,' one of them said, 'what were those ten things?' The grandmother smiled. 'To be quite honest about it,' she said, 'I never did get around to making that list. So every time Henry did something I didn't appreciate, I would simply say, "Lucky for him – that one is on the list."'[1]

Lucky for him he was married to her. A not so lucky husband described his wife as a one-woman grievance committee always in session. In marriage, as in life, it is easy to collect hurts and recite grievances, but true love works hard at keeping short accounts. According to Paul: 'Love keeps no record of wrongs' (1 Cor. 13:5). The verb used in this text is an accounting term, which means 'to credit to someone's account'. It is the picture of the bookkeeper turning the pages of his ledger, keeping tabs on all that has been received and spent. Paul's point is that love doesn't keep a black book on people and the wrongs they have done against us. It forgives and forgets. It blots out and wipes away the record of that injury or injustice. Chrysostom observed that a wrong done against love is like a spark that falls into the sea and is quenched.

This kind of love is to be a way of life for the Christian for a number of reasons. On the one hand, it is the only way to

---

1.   Fred Lowery, *Covenant Marriage* (West Monroe, LA: Howard Publishing Press, 2002), p. 220.

survive a broken world. We will be sinned against, even by those closest to us. Therefore, this kind of love is in a very real sense a matter of survival. We must keep short accounts if we are to prevent our souls from becoming acidic (Eph. 4:31-2). We must keep short accounts if we are not to forfeit today and tomorrow because we are a prisoner to yesterday's grievances (Phil. 3:13-14).

And on the other hand, this kind of love is the natural response of those who have been touched by the grace of God. The same Greek word that Paul employs in 1 Corinthians 13:5 to speak of love not keeping a record of wrongs is used often in the New Testament to represent the pardoning act of God toward those who put their trust in Christ's redeeming death. The record of our sin is put to Christ's account (Rom. 4:8; 2 Cor. 5:19). If God keeps no record on us, how can we as His children keep a record on others?

Bury the hatchet today, and don't leave the handle sticking up.

God, thank You for burying my sins at the bottom of the ocean.
Help me to forgive and forget as well.
In Jesus' Name, amen.

I Stand Corrected

It is better to hear the rebuke of the wise than for a man to hear the song of fools. For like the crackling of thorns under a pot, so is the laughter of the fool. This also is vanity.
(ECCLESIASTES 7:5-6)

A man was on the practice golf course when the club pro brought another man out for a lesson. The pro watched the man swing several times, and then began making some suggestions as to how the fellow could improve his game. But each time the pupil interrupted with his own version of what was wrong and how he could fix it. After a few minutes of this kind of exchange, the pro began nodding his head in agreement. At the end of the lesson, the student paid his teacher, thanked him for his advice, and left quite pleased with how things had gone. The observer was so astonished by what had transpired that he asked the pro, 'Why did you go along with him?' 'Son,' the old pro said with a grin as he pocketed his fee, 'I learned long ago that it is a waste of time to sell answers to a man who simply wants to buy echoes.'[2]

Like the man in our story, most of us would rather be ruined by praise than saved by constructive criticism. We would rather walk away from the truth about ourselves than stand corrected. But the Bible would remind us that it is better to be scolded by a wise man than serenaded by a fool (Eccles. 7:5-6). King Solomon had lived long enough to know that it is better to receive a meaningful slap in the face, so to speak, than to receive a meaningless slap on the back. There are plenty of people who will tell us what we want to hear, but their words are like the burning of thorns at a campfire. Their words make a lot of noise but no lasting good comes from them. It is the rebuke of the wise man that brings lasting benefit to our lives (Ps. 141:5). Faithful are the wounds of a friend who stings us with corrective criticism (Prov. 27:5-6).

This is a bad-tasting medicine. Many of us have an aversion to admonition because we have been on the wrong end of

---

2.   Haddon Robinson, *Decision Making* (Wheaton, IL: Victor Books, 1991), p. 114.

correction devoid of grace. Many of us have an aversion to admonition because we don't want to do the hard work of changing. Many of us have an aversion to admonition because we are blinded by pride and cannot see what others cannot miss. But like most bad-tasting medicines, the rebuke of the wise is worth swallowing (Prov. 10:17; 13:18; 25:12). The rebuke of the wise adds length to our life and depth to our days. You cannot laugh your way to maturity in life or in Christ.

Nobody likes a critic, and any fool can be a critic, but true and appropriate rebukes are really good wishes turned inside out, designed to mold and mature us in wonderful ways. One of the best ways to live and learn is to humbly receive the correction of others who themselves have been tempered by time and trained in truth. Friends and family don't exist simply to reinforce us, but to sanctify us, mature us, and act like sandpaper smoothing away those rough edges that have not yet been conformed to Christ.

God, thank You that You speak truth, even hard truth.
Help me to have ears to hear the negative for a positive purpose.
In Jesus' Name, amen.

Show Some Patience

Love suffers long and is kind; love does not envy; love does not parade itself, is not puffed up.

(1 CORINTHIANS 13:4)

Charles Simeon throughout his ministry fought the good fight of faith. He helped establish a beachhead for evangelical advance within the Church of England in the eighteenth century. From the early days of his ministry at Holy Trinity in Cambridge, his congregation opposed his ministry. Parishioners locked their pews and the churchwardens locked the doors. For some years Simeon, basically, preached to bare walls. Yet, the most fundamental conflict that Simeon had was with his own heart. He had a somewhat harsh and self-assertive air about him. One day, early in Simeon's ministry, he was visiting Henry Venn, who was a pastor twelve miles from Cambridge at Yelling. When he left to go home, Venn's daughters complained to their father about his pompous and prickly manner. Venn took the girls to the back yard and said, 'Pick me one of those peaches.' But it was early summer, and the peaches were still unripe. They asked why he would want the green, unripe fruit. Venn replied, 'Well, my dears, it is green now, and we must wait; but a little more sun, and a few more showers, and the peach will be ripe and sweet. So it is with Mr Simeon.'[3]

Like Charles Simeon people will try our patience, but we must see them, as did Henry Venn him, as unripened fruit. A little more patience, a little more kindness, and a little more understanding on our part can be used by God to sweeten the sour, win the lost, and mature the immature. Paul reminds us in 1 Corinthians 13:4 that 'Love suffers long.' Christian love, patterned after the cross of Christ, is patient and slow to anger. It is a disposition of spirit that doesn't boil over easily. It holds back and makes allowances for people's faults and failures. It is a love that puts up with a lot (Rom. 12:18).

Showing patience is God's will because it is God's way. God's love for mankind is patient and resilient (Ps. 103:8; Rom. 2:4;

---

3. Hugh Evan Hopkins, *Charles Simeon of Cambridge*, (Eugene, OR: Wipf & Stock, 1977), p. 101.

2 Pet. 3:8). Thankfully, God works with a long rope. God continues to hold out His hand to the rebel as in the days of the prophet Isaiah (Isa. 65:2-3). We worship a God who suffers the insufferable! We have a God who patiently loves those who are hard to love! Let us, therefore, extend to others that which we have so abundantly received from God ourselves. May we model God's patient love out of gratitude and obedience towards Him. But not only should we show some patience out of obedience, but also out of faith. Our patience toward others is to be motivated by faith towards God. Patience is not simply resignation in the face of imperfection, but an active waiting upon God to change that person, just as He did with Paul (1 Tim. 1:12-17). Showing patience is conformity to God, but it is also hope in God! Thomas Carlyle said, 'If you have a creed, you can afford to wait.' We do have a creed, and it is the gospel of God's patient love in Christ toward us. Therefore, we can afford to wait for God to change others.

God, thank You for waiting on me to ripen.
Help me also to wait on others to ripen.
In Jesus' Name, amen.

Pick Your Fights

Therefore, as the elect of God, holy and beloved, put on tender mercies, kindness, humility, meekness, longsuffering; bearing with one another, and forgiving one another, if anyone has a complaint against another; even as Christ forgave you, so you also must do. But above all these things put on love, which is the bond of perfection.

(COLOSSIANS 3:12-14)

President Theodore Roosevelt used to have a pet dog that was always getting into fights and being beaten by other dogs. A reporter once asked the president about that. The reporter stated, 'Your dog is not much of a fighter, is he, Mr President?' Roosevelt replied, 'That is not true. He is a wonderful fighter! He is just a poor judge of dogs.'

If there is a lesson to be learned from this story, it is the necessity of learning to pick your fights, to become a better judge of the things we want to fuss and fight over. Life provides us ample opportunity to be offended and many reasons to come out of our corner fighting. But wisdom would remind us that some things and some people are better left alone. Not every issue in life needs to become a Supreme Court or Grand Jury case. Not every fight is worthy or worth it. As the old saying goes, 'Anybody can whip a skunk; it is just not worth it.' We must fight the temptation to go through life in the objective case, picking the wrong fights, and getting heated over the wrong issues. The fact is that some things are a matter of forbearance, and some a matter of forgiveness.

That is a life lesson that Paul teaches us in his letter to the Colossians (Col. 3:12-14). It is clear from this text that not all offenses require forgiveness. Paul says: 'Bearing with one another, and forgiving one another, if anyone has a complaint against another; even as Christ forgave you, so you must also do' (Col. 3:13). Some things are a forbearance issue – things like personality differences, irritating mannerisms, immature blunders, and poor but well-intended decisions. Other things are forgiveness issues. The word 'complaint' employed by Paul carries the idea of something worthy of blame – something morally objectionable, something that violates some universal sense of justice, something bad enough to require forgiveness!

Some things are a matter of forbearance, not forgiveness. Some things and people are better lived with, than confronted. We must not go through life majoring on the minors. Our Lord warned us about the danger of getting things out of proportion by staring at gnats, while at the same time swallowing camels (Matt. 23:23-4). We need to learn to judicially hold our fire and pick our fights. We need to reserve forgiveness for those things that truly matter. The use and application of forgiveness is not unlike the use of an antibiotic. We don't use antibiotics to cure the common cold or deal with every germ that comes our way. Overuse would be to misuse. It is the same with forgiveness. Most of the germs that infect our relationships don't need anything as strong as forgiveness. They simply need to be overlooked and ignored (Prov. 19:11). Life is too short to have a very long list of things that are going to truly upset you.

God, I praise Your patience with me. I depend on You to help me
forbear the petty problems.
In Jesus' Name, amen.

Double Vision

One of the two who heard John speak, and followed Him, was Andrew, Simon Peter's brother. He first found his own brother Simon, and said to him, 'We have found the Messiah' (which is translated, the Christ). And he brought him to Jesus. Now when Jesus looked at him, He said, 'You are Simon the son of Jonah. You shall be called Cephas' (which is translated, A Stone).

(JOHN 1:40-2)

Leonard Bernstein, the great American composer, says that when he was young his father adamantly opposed his going into music. There was no 'strike up the band, and let's celebrate around the Bernstein home!' the day that Leonard entered music school. Reflecting on those early days Bernstein notes: 'If you were to ask my father today if he opposed this, he would not deny it, but he would rationalize, "How was I to know that he was a Leonard Bernstein?"'[4]

Anticipating what people may become is not an easy thing. It is hard sometimes to see the man in the boy, the professor in the slow learner, the overcomer in the failure, the beauty queen in the pimply girl, the friend in the enemy, and the saint in the sinner. But by God's grace people can far exceed our expectations. They can break through the ceiling we have set for them. When it comes to looking at people, we need double vision. We need to look beyond what they are to what they can become through the artistry of God's transforming grace.

In the Gospel of John, we are introduced to the double vision of Christ regarding Simon Peter. Jesus looks on Simon and tells him that he will be called Cephas, meaning the stone (John 1:40-2). Jesus sees Simon, the volatile fisherman, who is as unpredictable as the winds that sweep across the Sea of Galilee, but He also sees Peter, the rock-solid apostle, who will be a pillar in the early church (Gal. 2:9). In this change of name, we have the anticipation of future grace and the transformation of this

---

4.   Paul W. Powell, *The Saint Peter Principle* (Nashville, TN: Broadman Press, 1982), p. 16.

man's character. Peter is the pebble that became a rock. Jesus sees double! Jesus looks beyond the moment and the man and envisions what he will become. He knows how the story ends with God as its author. Jesus sees potential where others do not. No matter how Peter felt about himself, Jesus loved him and saw what he could be (2 Cor. 5:17). Christ changed Peter, and Peter changed the world.

The gospel of God's grace allows us to write people in, whom others write off. People can change and exceed our expectations. People tend to define themselves as we see them, therefore they deserve a second look. The German poet, Goethe, stated: 'Treat a man as he appears to be, and you make him worse. But treat a man as if he was what he potentially could be, and you make him better.' Just as it does not appear right now what we shall be when God is finished with us, so we need to remember that others can become what they are not right now (1 John 3:2). Anticipating future grace in another's life is the hallmark and hope of the gospel. There are diamonds to be found in the rough, if you will take a second look.

Today, give someone a second glance and chance.

You are the God who sees and sees double.
Help me to give others a second glance and chance too.
In Jesus' Name, amen.

Go Easy

If a man is overtaken in any trespass, you who are spiritual restore such a one in a spirit of gentleness, considering yourself lest you also be tempted. Bear one another's burdens, and so fulfill the law of Christ.

(GALATIANS 6:1-2)

John Wesley, the great Methodist evangelist, was once crossing the Atlantic on his way to America with Mr Olgethorpe, who was to be the governor of Savannah, Georgia. On one particular day during the voyage, Wesley heard a great commotion down in the governor's cabin. The fracas centered on the fact that Mr Oglethorpe's servant, Grimaldi, had drunk the governor's favorite bottle of wine. Wesley, who stumbled upon the situation, learned that the governor intended to have Grimaldi beaten on the deck and then put on the first warship that came by, where he would be pressed into His Majesty's service. When Wesley pleaded for some leniency, the governor replied, 'I never forgive.' Wesley immediately responded, 'Your honor, then I hope you never sin.' The rebuke was persuasive and pointed, causing the governor to stop in his tracks. With some humility, he said to Wesley, 'Alas, Sir, I do sin, and I have sinned in what I have said; for your sake he shall be forgiven; I trust he will never do the like again.'

That story is a gripping and good reminder to go a little easier on those we find caught up in sin. Since none of us are without sin, as Wesley reminded Mr Olgethorpe, we should not be so fast to cast the first stone (John 8:7). Yet, it is all too easy for us in a fit of rage or a wounded spirit to want to throw the book at someone, but in wanting to do so, we can forget the one true book itself, the Bible. In his letter to the Galatians, the apostle Paul reminds them and us, that we need to go easy with those who have been caught up in sin (Gal. 6:1-2). Paul encourages us to restore them with a gentle and humble spirit. We all know what it is to be tempted, and we all know what it is to sin. The fallen are to be restored, not ignored, not deplored. Those who are spiritual, that is those who are walking in the Spirit and bearing the fruit of the Spirit, must handle the bruised and broken with love, patience, and gentleness (Gal. 5:16-26). Those who are walking in the Spirit don't kick people when they are down. The word 'restore' in our text speaks of resetting a broken bone. The sinning brother is likened to a broken bone in the body of Christ, and as with broken bones, the process of restoration is a painful one and needs to be undertaken with compassion and care. The process of restoration is outlined for us in Matthew 18:15-17.

In dealing with the sinning brother, let us remember something F. B. Meyer, the English preacher, once said. He said, 'When we see a brother or a sister in sin, we should remember that there are three things we do not know: first, we do not know how hard he or she tried not to sin; second, we do not know the power of the forces that assailed him or her; and third we do not know what we would have done in the same circumstances.'[5]

Go easy on the fallen for their sake, your sake, and the gospel's sake!

God, You delight in mercy.
Help me to join You in binding up the bruised.
In Jesus' Name, amen.

---

5.   Peter Lewis, *The Lord's Prayer* (London: Hodder and Stoughton, 1995), p. 157.

Stop Making Comparisons

So Saul clothed David with his armor, and he put a bronze helmet on his head; he also clothed him with a coat of mail. David fastened his sword to his armor and tried to walk, for he had not tested them. And David said to Saul, 'I cannot walk with these, for I have not tested them.'

(1 SAMUEL 17:38-9)

An old Peanuts cartoon shows Lucy, Linus, and Charlie Brown stretched out on the grass, looking up at the clouds. 'What do you think you see, Linus?' asks Lucy. Linus motions toward the sky and answers, 'Well, those clouds up there look to me like the map of the British Honduras in the Caribbean. That cloud up there looks a lot like the profile of Thomas Eakins, the renowned painter and sculptor. And that clump of clouds over there gives me the impression of the stoning of Stephen. I can even see Saul standing there to one side.' Then Lucy asks, 'What do you see in the clouds, Charlie Brown?' Says Charlie, 'Well I was going to say I saw a duckie and a horsie, but I changed my mind.'[6]

As this story illustrates, the ideas, gifts, and, accomplishments of others can intimidate and distract us if we let them. The strengths of others can make us feel weak. The wealth of others can make us feel poor. The giftedness of others can make us feel hapless. And the wisdom of others can make us feel foolish. Thinking comparatively and competitively of others can leave us thinking less about ourselves and what God has called us to be and do. But God doesn't want us living out of someone else's suitcase. God wants us to be us for Him. You see that in Jesus' words to Peter (John 21:20-2). You see that in David's words to Saul (1 Sam. 17:38-9). God wants our uniqueness to define and direct us. As in the case of Saul's armor, what fits others doesn't necessarily fit us . Each of us is an original (Ps. 139:13-18). Each of us is uniquely gifted by the Holy Spirit (1 Cor. 12:11). And each of us has been given a distinct calling (Eph. 2:10). Therefore, each of us needs to be our best selves in Christ and for Christ.

---

6. Bryan Chappell, *Christ-Centered Sermons* (Grand Rapids, MI: Baker Academic, 2013), p. 41.

Remember, excellence is not being the best, but doing your best. We need to stop making comparisons. There is only one of you and one of me, so let's not rob God of His multifaceted glory, or this world of our unique contribution, by being less than our true selves. We need to stop making unhealthy and unholy comparisons with others, and here is how:

First, purpose to live the life God has planned for you. David served God's purpose in his generation (Acts 13:36). Paul died having finished the course God had mapped out for him (2 Tim. 4:6-8). As the old hymn puts it, 'There is a work for Jesus only you can do.'

Second, learn to rejoice in the success of others (Rom. 12:15). Loving your neighbor means rejoicing in God's love toward them in any advance that they might enjoy.

Third, cultivate the grace that wants for others what God may not desire for you. You see that graciousness and humility in John the Baptist as he willingly steps aside and lets Jesus come to the forefront (John 3:30).

Fourth, be mindful of the unpredictable nature of grace (Matt. 20:1-16, esp. 16). Making comparisons is antithetical to the doctrine of grace. Grace by its very nature is undeserved, indiscriminate, and radical. It defies convention, competition, and comparison, which means there are no winners and losers in grace, only those who are better off than they deserve. In grace everyone is a winner. Life begins by stopping making comparisons!

God, there is none like You (Isa. 45:6)!
Help me embrace the unique potential You have given to me.
In Jesus' Name, amen.

The Things that Make For Peace

I, therefore, the prisoner of the Lord, beseech you to walk worthy of the calling with which you were called, with all lowliness and gentleness, with longsuffering, bearing with one another in love, endeavoring to keep the unity of the Spirit in the bond of peace.

(EPHESIANS 4:1-3)

The story is told of the Irishman who went to his local priest for help regarding his marriage. He told the priest that his wife was a holy terror at home. She was incorrigible. She was like a volcano ready to explode at any moment. She would fly off the handle and curse up a storm. The parishioner asked the priest if he would be willing to come home with him and give his wife a stern talk. Although the priest was at first very reluctant to wedge himself into the middle of a domestic dispute, he agreed to go. After all, it was his parish duty! As they approached the house, the man told the priest to wait outside for a few minutes while he went inside. When the priest asked why? The man replied, 'Well, I need to go inside and get her started.'

The man in our story is more of the problem than he imagines, and so are we when it comes to many of our personal and professional conflicts. After all, it takes two to tango. James, the half-brother of our Lord Jesus, would remind us that conflict often arises out of wounded self-love or a spirit of covetousness and competitiveness (James 4:1-3). One man's fall into sin left all men with concaved hearts, hearts turned in on themselves, hearts that are self-seeking. Therefore, anyone or anything that competes with our desire for pleasure or preeminence is seen as a threat, a threat that must be eliminated, which invariably leads to conflict. Our problem with others really begins with us! Our self-centered desires, unmet expectations, and unyielding wills are often the genesis of our conflicts with people.

Sadly, starting a fight is too easy for us. We are good at it because we are bad. But stopping the fight is hard! That is why we would do well to heed the admonition of Paul to the Ephesians regarding the things that make for peace (Eph. 4:1-3).

In seeking to engender unity among them, Paul calls for grace and grit in the pursuit of peace.

First, harmony requires grace (Eph. 4:1-2). Conflict is primarily a sin issue, and therefore requires a gospel solution. Paul immediately calls upon the Ephesians to live out their relationship with Christ in relationship to others. They need to walk worthy of their calling in Christ. He wants the gospel to shape, deepen, and repair their relationships with each other. Why? Because the saving work of Christ not only brings people to God, it brings people together. Like the Savior, they must be marked by humility. They must put others before themselves. Like the Savior, they must be meek and show strength under control. They must not treat others rudely or roughly. Like the Savior, they must manifest a forbearing spirit toward those who would test their patience. They must make room for others to fail and live in the hope that people can change. We must do similarly!

Second, harmony requires grit (Eph. 4:3). Paul would have them and us know that conflict resolution is work. We must endeavor to diligently apply ourselves to keeping the peace. We must sweat to take the heat out of conflict. In the light of the gospel, we must take the initiative in building bridges of better communication and pulling down walls of misunderstanding.

Remember, the things that make for peace are grace and grit!

God, thank You for being the God who breaks down barriers
through Your cross. I need Your grace and grit
in the midst of conflict.
In Jesus' Name, amen.

Surviving
the Struggle to Pray More and to Pray Better

Keep on Knocking

So I say to you, ask, and it will be given to you; seek, and you will find; knock, and it will be opened to you. For everyone who asks receives, and he who seeks finds, and to him who knocks it will be opened.

(LUKE 11:9-10)

William Temple, ninety-eighth Archbishop of Canterbury, famously said, 'Prayer is not the overcoming of God's reluctance but the laying hold of His willingness.' In these words, we are reminded that we should never be afraid to pray to God or hesitate to ask for His help. God does not have to be cajoled into taking an interest in our interests. He is actually more willing to help us than we are to ask for His help (James 1:5). The Lord Jesus said: 'Ask and it shall be given to you' (Luke 11:9). God is not like one of those soda machines that you have to kick and bang to get anything from it.

Agreed, but that raises a question! If prayer is not the overcoming of God's reluctance, then why does Jesus tell His disciples to keep on asking, seeking and, knocking in prayer (Luke 11:9-10)? Why is there this persistent call in Scripture to persistence in prayer if God is so willing to answer our heart's cry (Luke 18:1; Col. 4:2)? I believe the answer to that question lies in the fact that persistence in prayer is about changing us, not God. It is our lack of faith that needs to be overcome, our mixed motives that need to be purified, and our ingratitude that needs to be challenged. Persistence in prayer helps us on these three fronts:

First, let us not forget that when we remain steadfast in prayer, our faith grows. Faith is like a muscle, and the more it is exercised, the stronger it grows. Prayer is an act of faith and persistent prayer is a stretching of our faith. After all, to pray once about a matter and then to forget it would be more a matter of presumption than prayer.

Second, let us not forget that persistent praying assists us in the process of determining the extent to which we truly desire and genuinely need what we are requesting of God. Good parents don't rush out and buy a particular toy the first time their child asks for it. Instead they allow time to go by to determine the depth of the child's desire and the genuineness of the need. God's love for us is just as discriminating, and so He has us ask again and again. This process keeps prayer from being seen as a magic wand.

Third, let us not forget that perseverance in prayer fosters a greater gratitude for God's provision when it finally comes. In a world of instant gratification and access to many things, we can often fail to appreciate what we have and what comes easily to us. We take things for granted, rather than with gratitude. As in life, so with prayer, that which is received after a time of waiting is generally greeted with greater thanksgiving.

Persistence in prayer is good for you and brings good to you! Therefore, keep knocking!

God, thank You that You are eager to lend an ear.
Help me to keep knocking, not to change Your mind but to
change mine.
In Jesus' Name, amen.

Lost for Words

Likewise the Spirit also helps in our weaknesses. For we do not know what we should pray for as we ought, but the Spirit Himself makes intercession for us with groanings which cannot be uttered. Now He who searches the hearts knows what the mind of the Spirit is, because He makes intercession for the saints according to the will of God. And we know that all things work together for good to those who love God, to those who are the called according to His purpose.

(ROMANS 8:26-8)

As a man was leaving church, he stopped to talk to his pastor and told him, 'Pastor, you are smarter than Albert Einstein.' The pastor blushed and replied, 'Smarter than Einstein? Einstein was one of the smartest men who ever lived. What makes you think that I am smarter than Einstein?' In answer the man said, 'Well, Einstein was so smart that when he spoke people could only understand five percent of what he said. When you speak people cannot understand anything you say.'

Lack of clarity and comprehension is not only a problem in preaching, but in praying also. Paul, in his letter to the Romans, acknowledges that there are times in the Christian life where there is a failure to communicate our hearts' desire to God in a given set of circumstances. We know we ought to pray, but there are days when we do not know what we ought to pray (Luke 18:1; Rom. 8:26). Life leaves us scratching our heads. We stand stir-crazy at some crossroads in life, not knowing what to ask from God. Our thoughts are all jumbled up, leaving us tongue-tied before the throne of grace.

In such cases, our garbled prayers are due to the fact that we live in a fallen world as finite creatures. This passage places a groaning Christian in the midst of a groaning creation (Rom. 8:20-3, 26). It is hard to know what to pray for in an upside-down world. Besides a fallen world, we are stumped by our own weakness, which shows our blindness towards the mystery of God's providence (Rom. 8:26). We don't know what is best for us, nor do we know what constitutes God's best.

Sometimes God's best can be a bad thing that works for good (Rom. 8:28). Because of our world and weakness, there are times that all we can do is sigh. Our prayers become nothing more than a whimper.

The good news of our text is that when you and I find ourselves lost for words, the Spirit of God, who causes us to pray in the first place, prays for us (Rom. 8:14-17, 26-7). The marvel of Romans 8 is that the Third Person of the Trinity is said to become our prayer partner. Our weak prayers trigger His strong prayers. When you and I are without words, the Spirit makes intercession for us with divine articulations or groanings too deep for words to our Father in heaven. Our groaning in a broken world produces His groaning on our behalf. He is indeed the 'divine paraclete' who has been called alongside to comfort us. Watch this! The Spirit of God knows us completely, and God knows the mind of the Spirit perfectly, therefore, that which we cannot put into words is presented to God according to the will of God by the Holy Spirit on our behalf (Rom. 8:27). Amazing! The Spirit fixes our prayers on the way up so that God hears our prayer made better.

It is good to know that God hears us even when we are without words.

God, thank You that You pray for me and with me.
Comfort me even in my loss for words.
In Jesus' Name, amen.

Ask and You Will Receive

If you then, being evil, know how to give good gifts to your children, how much more will your Father who is in heaven give good things to those who ask Him!

(MATTHEW 7:11)

The story is told of a time when a great Scottish preacher prayed in the morning service for rain. As he went to church in the afternoon, his little daughter said, 'Here is the umbrella, Papa.' The seasoned church leader looked quizzically and asked, 'What do we need it for?' His daughter replied, 'You prayed for rain this morning. Don't you expect God to send it?' Duly rebuked, the great preacher took the umbrella, and while they were coming home later in the day, they were glad to take shelter under it as they found themselves caught in a downpour.

This story reminds us that prayer must always be more than a matter of speech. It must be an act of faith. Prayer ought to be words spoken or thoughts directed to God in confident expectation that God will hear and answer us. The Lord Jesus taught us to pray with the great expectations, believing that God will give us what we ask and supply what we seek (Matt. 7:7-12). Prayer is not a game of hide-and-seek where we seek and God hides. We don't have to bargain with God. We can be direct and ask Him for what we need. This is what children do with their earthly fathers, and we ought to do the same with our heavenly Father who is good and gives what is good (Matt. 7:9-10; Ps. 19:68). God loves to answer prayer. If we will call upon God about the right things in the context of right living, He will answer us (Jer. 33:3; Isa. 58:9).

God loves answering prayer so much that sometimes He answers our prayers before we have even said them. Through the prophet Isaiah, God tells us that there are occasions when He will answer before we call (Isa. 65:24). Out of His wonderful grace, He anticipates and provides for our every need. He can do that since He knows what we need even before we speak our two cents' worth (Matt. 6:8). Not only does God answer our prayer before we speak, but while we speak (Isa. 65:24). The promise through Isaiah to God's people is that while we are still speaking

God is often already acting. Prayer is never a waste of time, and on occasions, God wastes no time in answering us. In Acts, we see God answering prayer immediately in the release of Peter from prison while the church was still praying (Acts 12:1-17). Let us not be behind the door in asking God to answer us on the day that we call (Pss. 138:3; 102:2). Finally, God often answers our prayers after we speak. In the case of Hannah, God answered her prayer for a son later (1 Sam. 1:19, 27). In such a case, faith must be exercised, not only in the asking, but in the waiting. Remember, in the light of God's remembrance of Hannah, that God's delays are not God's denials!

Ask and you will receive – sometimes before, even during, but most times after!

God, thank You that You hear me, so help me to talk to You.
In Jesus' Name, amen.

Don't be Afraid to Ask

You lust and do not have. You murder and covet and cannot obtain. You fight and war. Yet you do not have because you do not ask.

(JAMES 4:2)

The great Baptist preacher Adrian Rogers told of a time when he was a student pastor in the Indian River County area of Florida, a region known for its citrus growers. On one occasion, a deacon in the church gave him a rather generous helping of delicious oranges. Not able to eat them all at once, the young student pastor lugged them upstairs to his second-storey garage apartment and put them in a closet. One day not long after that, Adrian spied a young boy eyeing and then trying to steal an orange from a lonely orange tree in his backyard. He decided to let him, knowing full well that this was a sour-orange tree. In Florida, these trees are beautiful to the eye, but the fruit is bitter to the taste. This was a crime that definitely did not pay. Now the irony of the story is, as Adrian Rogers points out, that if the little fellow had simply asked Adrian for an orange, he would have received more than he could have imagined. He would have been loaded down with the best of oranges from Adrian's more than ample stash. Instead he left with a bitter taste in his mouth. He had not, because he asked not.[1]

According to the apostle James, the Christian can make a similar mistake. Instead of asking God for His best, or what is best, we experience the bitter fruit of our own scheming and wisdom. James puts it bluntly when he writes: 'We have not, because we ask not' (James 4:2). This text plainly points to the fact that many a Christian enjoys less than they could, because they pray less than they should. The best things in life come from God, and they are ours for the asking through our Lord Jesus Christ (James 1:17; Rom. 8:32). James writes: 'If a man lacks wisdom, let him ask of God, who gives to all liberally, and without reproach' (James 1:5). God is not going to find fault with

---

1. Adrian Rogers, *The Power of His Presence* (Wheaton, IL: Crossway Books, 1995), p. 136.

our prayers, big or small. Therefore, we are not to be afraid to boldly ask God for those things we know to be within His will (Heb. 4:14-16). After all, He is a God of overflowing goodness and mercy (Pss. 23:5; 145:7)! He is a God who can do more than we think, and give more than we ask (Eph. 3:20-1)! Although it is important to note that our asking must be marked by unwavering trust (James 1:5-8), right motives (4:1-3), confession of sin (5:16), righteous living (5:16), and deep-seated earnestness (5:17). This is the kind of praying that accomplishes much.

Reflect upon these words from C. H. Spurgeon. He writes: 'I breathe so many cubic feet of air in a year; I am afraid that I shall ultimately inhale all the oxygen which surrounds the globe.' Surely the earth on which the man would stand might reply, 'My atmosphere is sufficient for thee.'

Don't be afraid to ask, and don't be afraid to go big. God's oranges are succulent, sweet, and are to be found in great abundance.

> *God, thank You that You delight to provide.*
> *Help me to delight to pray.*
> *In Jesus' Name, amen.*

Free Speech

Let us therefore come boldly to the throne of grace, that we may obtain mercy and find grace to help in time of need.
(HEBREWS 4:16)

A friend of Martin Luther once said of the great Protestant Reformer, 'I overheard him in prayer, but good God, with what life and spirit did he pray! It was with such reverence, as if he were speaking to God, yet with such confidence as if he were speaking to his friend.'

Like Martin Luther, our prayers should be marked by confidence and candor. We do not need to parse our words or hide our feelings before God in prayer. There is a guaranteed right to free speech that the Christian enjoys through Christ as our Great High Priest. There is a boldness and honesty that ought to mark our conversation with God.

In the book of Hebrews, the Christian is encouraged to come boldly to the throne of grace, so that he finds grace to help in time of need (Heb. 4:16). This verse invites us to express a bold frankness in our talk to God. In secular Greek, the word 'boldly' was used to speak of free speech in the public arena. While in the private sphere, it carried the idea of candor and openness. Because Jesus has passed into the heavens for us, and because Jesus ever lives to make intercession for us, and because Jesus having purged our sins sat down at the right hand of the Majesty on high as our representative, we possess and enjoy a right to free speech before God (Heb. 9:24; 7:25; 1:1-3). We do not need to fear a slip of the tongue, which might put us in God's bad book. We do not need to hold back our feelings for fear of censorship. God knows everything there is to know about us, and He invites us to speak candidly (4:12-13). God is not going to be surprised or shocked by anything we say. Plus, Jesus understands our struggles, temptations, and questions, having lived our life (2:17-18). Christ had Himself cried out candidly to God in prayer during the days of his incarnation (5:7).

There's not a friend to us like the lowly Jesus. He understands our losses and how we can lose it sometimes. He is not offended by our questions. He is not taken back by our complaints. Our tears do not shock Him. If anything shocks Him, it might be our shyness and the suppression of our true feelings. As far as the Bible is concerned, praying honestly is as important as praying properly. The God of truth invites us to be truthful before Him in prayer. He wants us to be frank and free in our speech. He is big enough to absorb our complaints and secure enough to handle our questions. As Jerry Sittser notes in his helpful book *When God Doesn't Answer Your Prayer*: 'What God can't tolerate is a plastic saint, a polite believer, someone who plays a part but never gets inside the soul of the character. God prefers working with people who like to fight.'[2]

Feel free to be yourself before God in prayer. God wants to hear from the real you!

God, thank You that You are real and I can be real with You.
In Jesus' Name, amen.

---

2.   Jerry Sittser, *When God Doesn't Answer Your Prayer* (Grand Rapids, MI: Zondervan, 2003), p. 59.

Friends in High Places

*For Christ has not entered the holy places made with hands,
which are copies of the true, but into heaven itself, now to
appear in the presence of God for us; not that He should
offer Himself often, as the high priest enters the Most Holy
Place every year with blood of another. He then would have
had to suffer often since the foundation of the world; but
now, once at the end of the ages, He has appeared to put
away sin by the sacrifice of Himself. And as it is appointed
for men to die once, but after this the judgment, so Christ
was offered once to bear the sins of many. To those who
eagerly wait for Him He will appear a second time, apart
from sin, for salvation.*

(Hebrews 9:24-8)

In April 2001, in the midst of renewed fighting between Israel
and the Palestinians, a motorcade carrying the Security Service
Chief of Gaza came under a hail of bullets from IDF troops. In
a state of panic, the official called Yasser Arafat from his car for
immediate help. This started a chain reaction of phone calls
that involved Arafat calling the U.S. Ambassador, who in turned
called the U.S. Secretary of State, Colin Powell. Colin Powell
immediately got in touch with Ariel Sharon, the then Prime
Minister of Israel, who wasted no time in ordering the shooting
to stop at once. And it did.[3] Talk about the benefit of friends in
high places. The Security Chief's connections saved his life.

In a similar yet more significant fashion, the Christian has
connections in high places through Christ, who is said to have
entered heaven itself, now to appear in the presence of God for
us (Heb. 9:24). After His resurrection, the Bible tells us that Jesus
ascended to the right hand of God where He makes intercession
for us (Rom. 8:34). What a reality! Christ carried our sins to the
cross and then carried our humanity to the heights of God's
throne where He represents us (Heb. 2:17-18; 4:14-15; 10:19-22).
What is Christ doing now? He is sitting down as a reminder of

---

3. *More Perfect Illustrations*, compiled by editors of PreachingToday.
com (Wheaton, IL: Tyndale House Publishers Inc. 2003), p. 10.

His finished work of propitiation on the cross for us (10:11-12). He is enthroned in heaven expecting the complete and ultimate defeat of His enemies (10:13). And as we have just mentioned, He is interceding for those who will come to God through Him (7:25). Christ is not sitting on His hands in heaven today; they are clasped in prayer for us! While on earth, Christ finished the work of redemption through His death and resurrection, but today in heaven the ascended Christ carries on the unfinished work of interceding on our behalf.

What might that intercession look like? Perhaps Jesus' High Priestly prayer in John 17, the real Lord's Prayer, would begin to answer that question for us. John tells us that during His incarnation, Christ prayed not only for His immediate disciples, but all future believers (John 17:9, 20). For what did He pray? He prayed that they might be cared for by the Father and delivered from evil (vv. 11, 15). He prayed that they might be filled with His joy (v. 13). He prayed that they might be changed, comforted, and cleaned by His Word (v. 17). He prayed that they might be unified before a world marked by disharmony (vv. 21-3). He prayed that they might be in heaven with Him, beholding His restored glory (v. 24). He prayed that they might experience the divine and excelling love of God for them (vv. 23, 26). What a prayer! And the best thing about Jesus praying is that it's sure to be answered (11:42). His prayers are always within the will of God, and that gives us confidence about their efficacy on our behalf (1 John 5:14-15).

Whatever your problem, whatever your crisis, add your weak prayers to His strong prayers and let the peace of God stand garrison over your heart (Phil. 4:6-7). Don't panic! You have a Friend in high places who is working for you. Help is on the way!

Thank You, God, for Your finished and unfinished work
on my behalf.
In Jesus' Name, amen.

Surviving
the Struggle to Gain Perspective

The Test of First Impressions

For thus says the Lord God of Israel: 'The bin of flour shall not be used up, nor shall the jar of oil run dry, until the day the Lord sends rain on the earth.' So she went away and did according to the word of Elijah; and she and he and her household ate for many days. The bin of flour was not used up, nor did the jar of oil run dry, according to the word of the Lord which He spoke by Elijah.

(1 KINGS 17:14-16)

We say that a first impression can be a lasting impression, and indeed that is true. The first time we do something is often the most memorable. The first time we meet someone, we immediately begin to decide whether we like them or not. First impressions are indelible, and that is why they can also constitute a test of faith. Sometimes we allow first impressions to blind us to later possibilities or to cause us to give up in despair. First impressions may be lasting, but they are not always correct. The Christian must always remember not to allow what they see by natural perception to blind them to what faith may behold (2 Cor. 5:7; Heb. 11:1)

A good example of what I am talking about is to be found in the story of Elijah and the widow of Zarephath (1 Kings 17:8-16). God tells Elijah to go to Zarephath in Sidon, for He has commanded a widow to provide for Elijah there. When the prophet Elijah gets to the gates of the city, he meets the widow God has appointed to take care of his physical needs, but she is gathering sticks to cook her last meal in an attempt to simply delay the impending death of herself and her son. Climbing inside of Elijah's head, one wonders what his first impressions were of this whole scenario. Seems improbable, doesn't it? How can the prophet of God ask a widow to feed him when she is down to her last meal? But amazingly Elijah surmounts the test of first impressions. Trusting God's word, he proceeds to ask the woman to first feed him. The audacity of it! But God honors the faith of the prophet and the faith of the widow by performing the miracle of the bin of flour that was never used up and the jar of oil that never ran dry. Elijah passed the test of first impressions with flying colors.

Each of us will face the test of first impressions. The beginning of something is often the hardest. A new job, a new school, a new marriage, a new church, or a new ministry often presents some initial challenges that turn out to be greater than you anticipated or altogether different than you imagined. During this time we can be tempted to doubt, and therefore fall short of God's full blessing. We can be bullied into taking the path of least resistance, and get off track with God's will. Elijah didn't doubt or concede. He simply trusted God's word and waited to see God do what only God can do. He believed to see God's goodness, and so must we (Ps. 27:13).

When Adoniram Judson went to Burma (now Myanmar) as a pioneer Baptist missionary in 1813, it would be over six years before he saw his first convert. Today there are more than two million believers in Myanmar. Don't let first impressions be lasting impressions!

God, You can do the impressive, so help me to look beyond my
first impression.
In Jesus' Name, amen.

Don't Stop Thinking About Tomorrow

But the day of the Lord will come as a thief in the night, in which the heavens will pass away with a great noise, and the elements will melt with fervent heat; both the earth and the works that are in it will be burned up. Therefore, since all these things will be dissolved, what manner of persons ought you to be in holy conduct and godliness, looking for and hastening the coming of the day of God, because of which the heavens will be dissolved, being on fire, and the elements will melt with fervent heat? Nevertheless we, according to His promise, look for new heavens and a new earth in which righteousness dwells.

(2 PETER 3:10-13)

There is a sense in which the study of prophecy does for us what traveling into space has done for the scientific world. Scientists have learned much about our world by going outside it through space travel and looking back. They have learned things about the human body, weather patterns, and the location of natural resources, just to name but a few. These explorers have realized things which they would never have learned had they not broken free from an earthbound perspective! In a similar way, Bible prophecy carries us out into the future and gives a perspective on our world that we would otherwise not have. That perspective helps us make better sense of our day and the world we live in. This heavenly mindedness is intended to make us of greater earthly use.

As we have said, the Bible is constantly moving us beyond the moment we live in and the world that surrounds us. The Scripture teems with prophetic material about the end times, the Second Coming of Christ, and the long tomorrow that lies beyond momentary day! Prophecy occupies about one fourth of all Scripture, much of it related to the return of Christ to earth. It is a dominant theme in seventeen Old Testament books. Only three out of the twenty-seven New Testament books do not mention Christ's Second Advent. Interestingly, every chapter in First and Second Thessalonians closes with a reference to the impending return of Christ. Given the wealth of that material and the consistency of that focus, it is clear that the Bible does not want us to stop thinking about tomorrow. The present day must be lived, eagerly and expectantly, in the light of these future realities. And what we learn about the future must inform and transform all that we do today. As C. S. Lewis has said: 'Those who have done the most in this life are those who have thought the most about the next.'

Thinking about tomorrow's world should shape our thinking and direct our living in several ways. One, fulfilled prophecy should give us a greater confidence in the veracity of God's Word (Acts 13:32-5, 42-4). Two, the thought of Jesus' soon return should cause us to be serious about our walk with God (1 Pet. 4:7-9; 2 Pet. 3:11-13). Three, the study of prophecy gives us a backbone to endure trials (James 5:7-11). Four, the thought of future resurrection and the reunion of God's people, which takes place at the Rapture, brings hope to the bereaved and brokenhearted (1 Thess. 4:13-18). Five, prophecy assures us that the unjust persecution of the church will not go unpunished by God (2 Thess. 1:5-10). Six, prophecy excites our passion for Christ who is the spirit of prophecy (Rev. 1:1-3; 19:10). Seven, the truth of Jesus' soon return fans the flame of our evangelistic endeavors (Matt. 24:14).

Don't stop thinking about tomorrow! Take an interest in the future, for that is where you will spend the rest of your life.

God, You are the light of the world. Thank You for not leaving us
in the dark about the future.
In Jesus' Name, amen.

The Blessing of Not Knowing it All

For now we see in a mirror, dimly, but then face to face.
Now I know in part, but then I shall know just as I also am
known.

(1 CORINTHIANS 13:12)

The mother was waiting for her little girl to get off the bus after
her first day at school. When she got off the bus, the mother asked
her, 'What did you learn today?' The little girl replied, 'Nothing,
I guess. The teacher said I have to come back tomorrow.' Life
has a way of bringing us all back again and again to the reality
of our own ignorance. They say that ignorance is bliss, but it
is also a fact. There is so much about ourselves we have yet to
discover, so much about the world in which we live we have yet
to explore, and there is so much about the faith we profess that
we have yet to grasp. One of the ironies and irritations of life
is that the more we know, the more we know about the less we
know. Warren Wiersbe was right when he said: 'The wiser a man
becomes the more ignorant he knows himself to be.'

Paul acknowledges this struggle in his first letter to the
Corinthians. There he cites the fact that we see things imperfectly
as in a poor mirror and that our knowledge is partial and
incomplete (1 Cor. 13:12). Now while that is one of the burdens of
living in a fallen world this side of heaven, we often fail to look
past that handicap and consider the blessing of not knowing it
all. There are some upsides to only knowing in part.

First, it is good that we do not know it all, for it keeps us
humble. Knowledge has a way of making us proud (1 Cor. 8:1).
We think we are better than others because we know more than
others. Knowing that we know in part should make us easy to
live with and keep us from acting like we are God. It frees us up
not to have an opinion on everything.

Second, it is good that we do not know it all for it causes us to
take life one day at a time (Matt. 6:34). Imagine God showed you
the future – all that is going to happen in the next five years –,
it would be overwhelming and discombobulating. Not knowing
it all, however, helps us live life because it allows us to live retail
not wholesale.

Third, it is good that we do not know it all, for it makes us kinder towards others. Not knowing the whole story of a person's life should make us very slow to judge another's actions (1 Cor. 4:1-5). We only see a momentary snapshot. Not knowing it all should cause us to give people the benefit of the doubt. Not knowing it all should caution us when tempted to give glib answers to life's perplexing problems.

Fourth, it is good that we do not know it all for it presses us to trust the One who does know all things. Something we do know though is Someone. Despite our ignorance, God unerringly and unswervingly works *all* things together for our good (Rom. 8:28).

God, thank You that You know all things and that I don't.
In Jesus' Name, amen.

Caught in the Middle

So we built the wall, and the entire wall was joined together up to half its height, for the people had a mind to work.

(NEHEMIAH 4:6)

On New Year's Day, 1929, Georgia Tech and the University of Southern California played each other in the Rose Bowl. Late in the second quarter, Roy Riegels recovered a fumble for California, but in his excitement became confused and started running some sixty-nine yards in the wrong direction before he was tackled by his own teammate. The ensuing punt gave Georgia Tech a 2–0 lead. In the locker room at half-time, Roy Riegels sat in the corner with his face buried in his hands. Riegels was so distraught that he had to be talked into returning to the game for the second half. Nibs Price the coach said, 'Roy, get up and go back out there. The game is only half over.'

Roy 'Wrong Way' Riegels is not the only person to have faced the temptation to give up when the game is only half over. In the book of Nehemiah we find the story of the rebuilding of the walls of Jerusalem under Nehemiah's leadership (445-433 B.C.). The walls had been built halfway when the resolve and strength of the workers began to give way (Neh. 4:6, 10). They were exhausted by what they had done up to this point, and discouraged as they looked at what was left to do. Caught in the middle of this challenging project, their commitment began to crumble. Nehemiah had to remind them that the game was only half over and that faith in God would see them through to victory (Neh. 4:14, 20). If God was for them, it didn't matter who or what was against them (Rom. 8:31, 37).

Half time can be a dangerous time. There in the middle, you neither have the initial booster rockets of early enthusiasm nor the pulling power of seeing the finish post. Have you noticed that it is halfway through your car payments that the shine of that new car has truly worn off? Have you noticed that it is halfway up the hill that the kids want to turn back down the hill? Have you noticed that it is in the middle years of life that you feel lost? Half time is a crying and trying time, and it makes us vulnerable to discouragement and failure.

At such times we must not become weary in well doing (Gal. 6:9). At such times we need to remember the patience of Job (James 5:11). At such times we need to run the race with endurance, looking unto Jesus the author and finisher of our faith (Heb. 12:1-4). Meadowlark Lemon, the old Harlem Globe Trotter star, said, 'The most useless statistic in sports is the half-time score.' More than one game has been won in the second half. So, get up, the game is only half over!

God, thank You that You meet me in the middle.
Give me stamina to finish the race.
In Jesus' Name, amen.

New Horizons

... and declared to be the Son of God with power according to the Spirit of holiness, by the resurrection from the dead.

(ROMANS 1:4)

Traveling by train within the Unites States, Bishop William Quayle fell into conversation with some of his fellow passengers. The bishop was not wearing his religious garb at the time, and so one of the passengers was curious to know what he did for a living. 'What is your line of business?' he inquired. After a moment's reflection, the bishop replied, 'Horizons!' He was right. Everyone who believes and proclaims the gospel of the Risen Christ travels and trades in 'horizons'.

In Romans 1:4, Paul affirms that Jesus was 'declared to be the Son of God with power according to the Spirit of holiness, by the resurrection from the dead.' The word 'declared' is strikingly picturesque. This is the Greek word from which we get our English word 'horizon,' which basically means 'to distinguish'. The horizon is a line separating heaven from earth. Just as a horizon serves as a clear dividing line between land and sky, the resurrection of Christ distinguishes Him from the rest of humanity, declaring Him to be the Son of God.

The resurrection provides us a new horizon of understanding regarding the person and work of Christ. Christ's resurrection on the third day shows that He is divine (Rom. 1:4), that He has paid for our sins (1 Cor. 15:17), that He has defeated death (Acts 2:24), and that He is the procurer of eternal life for those who trust in Him (John 11:25-6). It led to His ascension and present heavenly enthronement (Acts 2:32-4; Phil. 2:9-11). It also anticipates His return to earth in a moment of glorious vindication and victory (Acts 1:9-11; 1 Pet. 1:3-5; Rev. 1:7). No wonder the doctrine of the resurrection is the capstone in each Gospel! If the death of Christ is the heart of the gospel, then the resurrection is the vascular system that carries life and vitality to the whole body.

The resurrection not only offers us a new horizon on Christ, but many new horizons regarding our own lives. In the resurrection of Jesus, God introduced a new dynamic into the course of human experience. It provides our faith a historical foothold. We believe certain things to be true because a certain event did happen. Our faith and hope rests in a divine Galilean whose lungs filled with oxygen again (Acts 1:1-3).

The resurrection also unleashes a triumphant spirit within life. For the Christian, new life is not just a future goal; it is a present experience (Eph. 2:5). The power that raised Jesus from the dead is at work in us leading us in a victory lap through life (Phil. 3:10; Heb. 13:20-1).

And finally, the resurrection offers us hope in the face of death. Christ's own resurrection has turned the grave into a thoroughfare rather than a dead end. Death actually issues in a greater experience of life (John 14:19; 11:25-6). Remember today that the resurrection is far from being something we only benefit from in the future. It is our constant horizon.

God, thank You for Your resurrection.
It brightens my present and my future.
In Jesus' Name, amen.

Points of Reference

'For I am the LORD, I do not change; Therefore you are not consumed, O sons of Jacob.'

(MALACHI 3:6)

In reply to a delegation of bank presidents suggesting to Abraham Lincoln whether it was time or not to give up all thought of the Union, the president told the following story:

> When I was a young man in Illinois, I boarded for a time with the deacon of a Presbyterian church. One night I was aroused from my sleep by a rap at the door, and I heard the deacon's voice exclaiming, 'Arise Abraham! The Day of Judgment has come!' I sprang from my bed and rushed to my window and saw stars falling in great showers; but, looking back of them in the heavens, I saw the grand old constellations, with which I was so well acquainted, fixed and true in their places. Gentlemen, the world did not come to an end then, nor will the Union now.[1]

As Abraham Lincoln proves, it is a good thing to be able to get your bearings from some fixed points of reference in a world that is constantly turning and churning. Life is forever in flux, and therefore, you and I need anchor points that will steady our faith and calm our nerves.

Reference point number one is the person of God. In a world that changes by the minute, we can focus our faith on the immutable nature of God (Mal. 3:6; Heb. 13:8). God does not atrophy or age (Ps. 102:24-7). His love for us is unchanging (Rom. 8:35-9). His mercies toward us are new every day (Lam. 3:22-3). As A. W. Tozer notes: 'God cannot change for the better, for He is perfect, and being perfect, He cannot change for the worse.'

Reference point number two is the promise of God. In a world of broken promises and shattered dreams, we can focus our faith on the eternal Word of God (Isa. 40:8; Matt. 24:35; John 6:68). The psalmist tells us that God's Word is forever settled in heaven

---

1. Anthony Gross (ed.), *The Wit and Wisdom of Abraham Lincoln* (New York, NY: Fall River Press, 1994), p. 189.

(Ps. 119:89). God's Word never ceases to be true, trustworthy, or timely. Because the Bible is unchanging, it has been said that a man with a Bible could stay in a cave for a year and at the end of that time, he could know what everybody else in the world was doing.

Reference point number three is the providence of God. In a world that is spinning out of control, we can focus our faith on the unstoppable will of God (Eph. 1:11). Whatever man does, God does something with it, even that which does not conform to His moral will (Prov. 16:9; 19:21; 21:1, 30-1). God has His providential hand on the tiller of history. God's sovereignty is the Christian's North Star. Whatever is going on in your world, always remember that God, His Word, and His plan are still in their places!

God, You are my constant point of reference.
I am relieved that Your character does not change
even though I find myself in changing circumstances.
In Jesus' Name, amen.

Precious Memories

The LORD is my light and my salvation; Whom shall I fear? The LORD is the strength of my life; of whom shall I be afraid? When the wicked came against me to eat up my flesh, my enemies and foes, they stumbled and fell. Though an army may encamp against me, my heart shall not fear; though war may rise against me, in this I will be confident.

(PSALM 27:1-3)

Any visit to Washington D.C. would be incomplete without a stroll along Massachusetts Avenue, where you pass roughly fifty foreign embassies housed in mansions that range from the elegant, to the imposing, to the out there. Many consider the four-acre British Embassy the crown jewel of the row. It was designed by Sir Edwin Lutyens to combine the offices and the residence of the ambassador, and it resembles an English country house in the Queen Anne style of architecture. Interestingly, this beautiful 1928 redbrick mansion has a statue of the bold and brilliant wartime leader Sir Winston Churchill out front, with one foot placed on British soil, and the other planted in the USA just outside the embassy property line.[2] The statue was erected as a wonderful symbol of Churchill's Anglo-American descent and the solidarity between these two great allies.

The statue of Churchill straddling the property line of the British Embassy in Washington D.C. says something to us. It teaches us how to fight fear. We must fight with one foot in the present and one foot in the past. Churchill once said, 'The further back you look, the further forward you will see.' Remembering what God has done for us in days gone by steels our nerves in the face of threatening enemies or events. Remembering God yesterday helps us handle our problems today.

In Psalm 27 we see David do this very thing. David arms himself in his fight with fear with the knowledge of God's past actions. Those who came to devour his life stumbled and fell (v. 2). That is a historical fact. In the light of that victorious

---

2. Steve Farrar, *Tempered by Steel* (Sisters, OR: Multnomah Publishers Inc., 2002), p. 89.

backdrop, David imagines further battles with the same outcome (v. 3). Verse two is the language of reflection, while verse three is the language of anticipation. David believed to see the goodness of the Lord in the future because he had seen the goodness of the Lord in the past (vv. 13-14). God had been with Him, and would be with Him. God's past faithfulness was the reason for David's present fearlessness (vv. 1-3).

Listen! Faith is well served by a good memory (Ps. 77:9-12; Lam. 3:21). However, if not directed properly, our memory can be treasonous. By a strange perversity, our mind collects hurts and fails to remember God's goodness and mercy. That is why we must not neglect the work of keeping the memory of God's past faithfulness alive so that we live to fight another day.

When a bloodhound has lost the scent of its prey, it usually works backward to find it again, and having found it, re-engages the hunt with renewed expectation and energy. So it is with the Christian who has been stopped in their tracks with paralyzing fear! Hope in God can be found again by thinking backward until faith is rediscovered and renewed. As Bob Jones Sr. once said, 'We must not forget in the dark what God taught us in the light.'

God, thank You for Your perfect track record.
Let Your faithfulness grow my faith.
In Jesus' Name, amen.

Small is a Big Deal

He who is faithful in what is least is faithful also in much;
and he who is unjust in what is least is unjust also in much.
(LUKE 16:10)

In the fall of 1865, the faculty of the fledgling Southern Baptist Seminary in Greenville, South Carolina, became burdened for more preachers of the gospel to help heal the nation's gaping wounds in the wake of the Civil War. To that end, John Broadus carefully prepared a seminary course on homiletics. To his surprise and sadness, only one student – a blind man – enrolled in the class. Nevertheless, Broadus determined, 'I shall give him my best, and I shall pursue my lectures as planned.'

Broadus delivered his lectures as planned to his solitary sightless student. The lectures were so long, and the material so rich that they were published in 1870. Of this book, David Dockery has noted: 'For decades it was the most widely used book on homiletics in the world. The volume, *On Preparation and Delivery of Sermons*, is still employed today in some settings. The publication of the volume evidenced God's providential oversight. Here was a book that came about through lectures to one blind student, in a small, at that time almost anonymous, institution in Greenville, South Carolina.'[3]

This story would remind us that little is much and can become much when dedicated to God. Nothing is small that is done for God. Therefore, it is an important lesson in life that you and I learn to make a big deal about small things. Jesus Himself taught us on a number of occasions that faithfulness in small things is a big thing.

In a number of His parables, Jesus employed a common proverb of the day, that faithfulness in small things leads to greater things (Luke 16:10; 19:17; Matt. 25:21). What holds true in the world of men also holds true within the kingdom of God. People who do small things well will be given greater

---

3. Timothy George and David S. Dockery (eds), *Theologians of the Baptist Tradition* (Nashville, TN: Broadman & Holman Publishers, 2001), p. 96.

responsibility and rewards! The Son of God would have us know that it is the hidden, menial, common, and small things done well that signals greatness and prepares us for the greater tasks. If David had never tackled the bear and lion, he would never have beaten Goliath from Gath (1 Sam. 17:33-6). While small things deserve to be done well for their own sake, they are nevertheless the proving ground for greater things (1 Tim. 3:10). The great souls are those who are faithful in that which is least.

In the trenches and tedium of daily living, we need to remember to make a big deal about small things. First, we must not despise small things (Zech. 4:10). Every great person started out as a small person. Every great invention started out as a small idea. The small things are still God's things, and He expects our best (Eccles. 9:10). Second, we are not to wait for some great work to drop in our lap. Do some little thing for God, and who knows what it may lead to (Luke 16:10)? Make every occasion a great occasion because God is watching. Small is a big deal!

God, You are a big God who uses even the small things.
Help me to do the small things well.
In Jesus' Name, amen.

That's Upside Down

But when they did not find them, they dragged Jason and some brethren to the rulers of the city, crying out, 'These who have turned the world upside down have come here too.'

(ACTS 17:6)

Tom Landry, famed coach of the Dallas Cowboys, was once quoted as saying something like: 'I have a job to do that is not very complicated, but it is difficult. It is to get a group of men to do what they don't want to do, so they can achieve the one thing they have wanted their whole lives.'[4] Discipline is the key to success on the sports field. And although it sounds upside down, victory is secured by getting players to do what they don't want to do, so that they might achieve what they have always wanted. In this seemingly contradictory statement, Coach Landry reminds us that success in life is often a matter of paradox. To get what you want, you often have to do what you don't want. In the spiritual realm, it is not any different.

Success and progress in the Christian life is often a matter of holy contradictions. God's kingdom is an upside-down kingdom when set against the world's thinking and formulas (Rom. 12:1-2). The kingdom of God is a counterculture that challenges our intuition and reverses our values. That is why the wisdom of God displayed in the cross of Christ is foolishness to the world (1 Cor. 1:18-31; 2:6-16). Those early Christians turned the world upside down because Christ had called them to an upside-down pattern of living (Acts 17:6). The fact is that the gospel upsets and inverts the normal pattern of things. God's ways are not our ways (Isa. 55:8-9). In God's kingdom you live by dying (Matt. 10:39)! In God's kingdom the way up is down (Matt. 23:12)! In God's kingdom foolishness brings wisdom (1 Cor. 3:18)! In God's kingdom weakness produces strength (2 Cor. 12:7-10)! In God's kingdom slow is fast (Isa. 40:31)! In God's kingdom to give is to have (Luke 6:38)! In God's kingdom little is much (John 6:9)!

---

4. Charles R. Swindoll, *Come Before Winter* (Portland, OR: Multnomah Press, 1985), p. 303.

And in God's kingdom you lead by serving (Luke 22:26). We must realize afresh that the truths of Christianity are often working through opposing forces. In God's kingdom opposites attract. Let us not forget that God took an instrument of death – a cross – and created a new order of life.

Listen to these challenging words by Tozer:

> A real Christian is an odd number anyway. He feels supreme love for One whom he has never seen, talks familiarly every day to Someone he cannot see, expects to go to heaven on the virtue of Another, empties himself in order to be full, admits he is wrong so he can be declared right, goes down in order to get up, is strongest when he is weakest, richest when he is poorest, and happiest when he feels worst. He dies so he can live, forsakes in order to have, gives away so he can keep, sees the invisible, hears the inaudible, and knows that which passes knowledge.

Think about that! The Christian life doesn't add up unless you remember that the Christian is an odd number anyway. Therefore, in a world that is back to front, you and I have got to find the courage to live lives that are upside down.

God, thank You for turning my life upside down.
Help me to follow in the footsteps of Your disciples.
In Jesus' Name, amen.

Not Half Bad

For I consider that the sufferings of this present time are not worthy to be compared with the glory which shall be revealed to us.

(ROMANS 8:18)

Not long ago I found myself sitting outside my local car wash waiting for my car to get dried and polished off. The car wash attendants were hard at work returning our vehicles to their pristine look. It was a beautiful day. The sun was shining. The sky was blue. And there wasn't a cloud in the sky. As I was waiting, I noticed this man being called to his car for pick up. It was a Mini Cooper S, and there it sat glistening like a jewel under a blazing sun for all to admire. But instead of getting into the vehicle, the man proceeded to walk around every inch of the car like a general inspecting his troops. He then started to nitpick and have the car wash attendants go back over some parts of the car polishing some more. After some more pouting and pointing, he eventually got into his car and drove off. As I watched the sorry scene, I thought to myself, now here is a guy who is going to have some major challenges in life. Here is a guy who is expecting too much. Here is a guy looking for perfection. As far as I was concerned, the car looked great before he inspected it, and the man seemed to have forgotten that as soon as he takes it back on the road it is going to get dirty in a hurry. He might even become a victim of a flock of birds on a bombing run. To be honest, as he drove off, I turned my head towards heaven and called in an air strike.

The point of this story is to remind us all that this man's approach to car washing is a bad philosophy on life. If you are looking for perfection, life will disappoint you. Life cannot meet that demand. The Bible tells us that this is a fallen world. We live among the ruins of a once glorious kingdom now spoilt by sin (Gen. 3:1-19). Life, because of Adam's disobedience, is only a pale reflection of what it once was (Rom. 5:12). Men, in all that they do, fall far short of God's glory (Rom. 3:10-18, 23). This planet and its inhabitants have been subject to futility following the Fall (Rom. 8:18-25). We are therefore to strive and settle for the possible, not the perfect (Rom. 12:18). Life must not be oversold. Greater joy is experienced in life when we lower our expectations. That last statement is not a call for mediocrity, but it is a call to biblical realism regarding the nature of life in a fallen world. There is a happiness and consolation to be gained in appreciating life's limitations. When you expect less, you enjoy more.

In the light of the doctrine of the Fall, we need to accept the fact that life is good when it is not half bad. We need to be less Pollyannaish, and more Pauline! Given the fallen nature of the world, we need to look at the glass as half full, not half empty. In fact, to speak biblically, we should see our cup as overflowing (Ps. 23:5). That which is not half bad in a bad-boy world is a good thing, and something to be enjoyed and celebrated. Few things are perfectible this side of heaven, so enjoy what you can. Let's be more realistic about the way we are, and the world is! Please, get in the car!

God, You're the only One I can rely on to be perfect.
Help me to accept the imperfections of this brief life.
In Jesus' Name, amen.

Identity Theft

*For in Him dwells all the fullness of the Godhead bodily; and
you are complete in Him, who is the head of all principality
and power.*

(COLOSSIANS 2:9-10)

Do you know what the fastest growing crime in America is? It is
identity theft with over 9.9 million incidents per year. According to
the *Wall Street Journal*, in 2012 alone, 7 percent of people sixteen
or older were identity theft victims. Credit card, bank account,
and other existing account use comprised 85 percent of the issues,
but people who suffered from new accounts being opened in their
name were more likely to suffer from serious financial, credit, or
emotional distress. Sadly, our society is awash with a crime wave of
identity theft, and so we need to guard our personal information
as well as double down on our computer security.

Having said that, there is another form of identity theft
that should concern us even more, and that is the theft of our
identity in Christ. To have our bank account rifled is one thing;
to be robbed of our riches in Christ is quite another. You and
I are always living out of some sense of identity. We are the son
or the daughter of someone. We are married to so-and-so. We
belong to such and such a team or club. This or that company
employs us. These connections give shape to who we are, and
how we perceive ourselves tends to mold how we act. How we see
ourselves in connection with others is a big factor in determining
the quality of our lives. It is the same in the Christian life.

One of the great emphases of the New Testament writers
is on the need to find one's identity in Christ. The apostles
were constantly reminding the early Christians of what they
had become in Christ and who they now were in Christ. They
were the elect, holy, and beloved (Col. 3:12). They were God's
workmanship (Eph. 2:10). They were new creations (2 Cor. 5:17).
They were heirs to the wealth of God's kingdom (Rom. 8:17). They
were the adopted sons and daughters of God (Rom. 8:15-16).
They were redeemed and forgiven (Eph. 1:7). They were citizens
of heaven (Phil. 3:20). They were complete in Christ (Col. 2:8-10).
They were righteous before God (1 Cor. 6:11; 2 Cor. 5:21).

Given those glorious realities, it is imperative that we live on a daily basis out of that sense of Christian identity. We must unite our thinking and behavior to the wonderful truth of our union with Christ (Rom. 6:1-14). That is what Paul is driving at when he tells the Romans to put on the Lord Jesus (Rom. 13:14). We need to clothe our self-image and dress our thoughts every hour around our identity in Christ. We must see ourselves as God sees us in Christ. We must accept ourselves for who God says we are. We must not let feelings, circumstances, or other people's opinions of us shape or define our fundamental understanding of who we are.

Upon the death of the late Duke of Windsor, who died in Paris in May 1972, the BBC immediately aired a documentary of the late royal reflecting on his upbringing as a boy. Looking back to his boyhood he said, 'My father [King George V] was a strict disciplinarian. Sometimes when I had done something wrong, he would admonish me saying, "My dear boy, you must always remember who you are."' So must we!

God, thank You for the glorious identity I have in Christ.
Guard me against identity theft.
In Jesus' Name, amen.

I Have A Dream

And you, who once were alienated and enemies in your mind by wicked works, yet now He has reconciled in the body of His flesh through death, to present you holy, and blameless, and above reproach in His sight if indeed you continue in the faith . . .

(COLOSSIANS 1:21-3)

In one of his last books on the subject of hope, Lewis Smedes tells how the great civil rights leader Martin Luther King kept hope alive for millions amidst the degradation and abuse of individual and institutional racism. He did this by setting the sights of his followers on a better day. He helped them imagine a land where people were 'not judged by the color of their skin, but by the content of their character.' On August 28, 1963, King gathered a quarter of a million people at the Lincoln memorial in Washington to appeal to the conscience of America. The country was at boiling point, and so the authorities counseled him to keep his rhetoric cool. Dr King agreed and proceeded to give a rather tame speech designed to turn the temperature down.

The story goes, as Smedes tells it, that the gospel singer, Mahalia Jackson, was sitting behind the great leader, and was beginning to become agitated at how flat the tone of the speech was. As the great civil rights leader was wrapping his speech up and about to sit down, she shouted out to him, 'The dream Martin, the dream – tell them about the dream . . . tell them about the dream!' At that precise moment Dr King launched into those now famous words, 'I have a dream, that one day on the red hills of Georgia, the sons of former slaves, and the sons of former slave-owners will be able to sit down together at the table of brotherhood ... '[5]

In Colossians 1:20, Paul tells the Christians at Colosse his own version of the dream. His dream, based on the reconciling work of Christ on the cross, envisions a world at rest and a world at

---

5. Greg Haslam (ed.) *Preach the Word* (Lancaster, UK: Sovereign Word Ltd, 2006), p. 121.

peace with God and itself. It's regarding a time at the end of time when there will be heaven on earth, a period when paradise is regained (Rev. 21:1-8)! It's a world marked by health, harmony, holiness, and happiness! Throughout this chapter, Paul has shown Christ to be the creator of the original earth (Col. 1:15-17) and the progenitor of a new humanity, the church, (Col. 1:12-14, 18, 21-2), but now Paul presents Christ as the architect of a new heaven and a new earth (Col. 1:19-20). Through what Christ did on the cross, the creation will be renewed and restored in the future. Christ's work of reconciliation not only makes things right with God and man, but with heaven and earth. As Paul explains, and extols the accomplishments of Jesus' death on the cross, the sweep of his thinking stretches beyond a few elect souls enjoying salvation to a creation at rest in Christ. Just as nothing of the fullness of God escapes Christ, so nothing in this world is beyond His reconciling work.

As we walk amidst the glorious ruins of this fallen world, it is a wonderful thought to imagine a world no longer savaged by extreme weather, a world where the lion will lie down with the lamb, a world where people are no longer the victims of disease and death (Rom. 8:18-22; 2 Pet. 3:13).

This is not an abandoned world! Life is not futile when viewed from a hill called Calvary! Amidst the ugliness of life on earth now, we need to tell ourselves that dream, and tell others that dream!

God, thank You for the speech You gave about a better future.
Help the dream of it to drive me now.
In Jesus' Name, amen.

Surviving
the Struggle to Rekindle Passion

Complacency Is A Killer

It happened in the spring of the year, at the time when kings go out to battle, that David sent Joab and his servants with him, and all Israel; and they destroyed the people of Ammon and besieged Rabbah. But David remained at Jerusalem.

(2 SAMUEL 11:1)

While I was ministering at Emmanuel Baptist Church in Toledo, Ohio, there was a man in our congregation who was a senior pilot with Northwest Airlines. He was among their top ten senior pilots and had some thirty years of flying the Boeing 747 around the world. One day over lunch Jim told me that there were three things that would kill a pilot and those under his charge and care. I was all ears! The first was fatigue, the second was distraction, and the third was complacency.

Complacency is indeed a killer, and not just in the field of aviation. Not paying attention to our walk with God, and not being vigilant about the spiritual dangers that surround us each and every moment, can be deadly. If we are not careful, we can in one moment sully the achievements of a lifetime. We are never more than one step away from a series of steps that could ruin our lives and legacy. King David is a bad and sad example of this very thing.

In 2 Samuel 11:1-27, we read the sordid tale of David's twin sins of adultery and murder. As a consequence, the rod, or in this case the sword of God's discipline, would never depart from David's house (2 Sam. 12:10). Chapter eleven is a depressing tipping point in the book. The first half of the book is a record of King David on his way up while the second half of the book is a chronicle of King David on his way down. Of interest to us is that this tipping point in the book centers on a time of complacency in David's life. David's slide into adultery and murder begins in the text with a reference to David loitering around Jerusalem. According to the narrator, it was the springtime when kings go off to war, but David was in his pajamas instead of his army fatigues (2 Sam. 11:1). David's staying back in Jerusalem is clearly identified in the text as something unusual. The narrator tells us where he thinks David should be. While Joab and the men of Israel are killing and being killed, David is killing time in Jerusalem, which will prove deadly as the text goes on to show. As David lingers, he spots a beautiful woman bathing and as they say, the rest is history. Materially and metaphorically speaking, David had taken his armor off and was a sitting duck for temptation and the tempter.

In the fight against sin and Satan, the Christian cannot take a day off. We must watch and pray lest we enter into temptation (Matt. 26:41). We must watch against prayerlessness. We must watch against pride and conceit. We must watch against bitterness and unforgiveness. We must watch against false doctrine. We must watch lest we fall (1 Cor. 10:12). Don't be hanging a welcome sign out for sin or Satan because of a lack of soul care and vigilance. An old friend in Northern Ireland used to say, 'Backsliding is slack abiding.' Snooze and you lose (Prov. 24:30-4).

God, thank You for candid warnings in Scripture.
Help me to stay on my tip toes.
In Jesus' Name, amen.

Lost That Lovin' Feeling

Nevertheless I have this against you, that you have left your first love.

(REVELATION 2:4)

When I was at The Master's Seminary training for the ministry, one of our professors, Jim Rosscup, who taught Bible Exposition, told us of his freshman year at Dallas Theological Seminary when beginning his theological training. He told us of feeling intimidated by the knowledge of other students in the class who had come to DTS straight out of Bible College. Jim had come to the school from an engineering background and found it all so new. So, in those early days, he opened up to his teacher about his struggle. Jim shared with Dr Howard Hendricks how it was all so new and rather overwhelming. Hendricks replied, 'Jim, let's hope it never becomes old.'

That is a good word and warning to all of us, is it not? Christians must ever be on guard against the erosion of their excitement and enchantment with Christ and the things of God, of their love for the Lord Jesus growing cold and stale, or of their passion for the eternal normalizing (Matt. 24:12)! It is a sad day when grace is no longer amazing. This was certainly a problem among the Ephesian Christians towards the end of the first century. In a letter to them, Christ takes issue with their lack of love for Him (Rev. 2:4). They were doing many good things. They were diligent in service, patient in suffering, and orthodox in doctrine (Rev. 2:2-3). But the problem was that they were doing those good things without doing the truly greater thing, which was to love Christ (1 Cor. 13:13). Over time their Christianity suffered from a creeping separateness from Christ. They were busy in the church, yet falling out of love with Christ the head of the church. Routine and predictability marked their walk with God and their work for Christ. Things had to change.

In a series of three terse commands, the Lord Jesus seeks to reset and rekindle this dying relationship (Rev. 2:4-5). First, they needed to *remember*. Christ called this church to recall the very beginnings of grace and the charm of God's love that once captured their hearts. Second, they needed to *repent*. Christ called this church to make an about-face and leave the sloping path that was taking them further and further away from first love commitment to Christ. Having recalled what was once good, they must immediately reject that which is less than the original good. Third, they needed to *repeat*. Christ called this church to replicate those early and extreme acts of devotion that often mark the first flush of love. He wants to see a honeymoon type love for God in action – a love that is free, pure, and reckless.

Have your prayers become predictable, your worship joyless, your reading of Scripture stale? Is it all becoming old? Then it's time to get back to a first love for the One who first loved us (1 John 4:19). Remember, repent, and repeat!

God, it is Your great love that motivates my love.
Help me to remember, repent, and repeat
so that I can fall back in first love with You.
In Jesus' Name, amen.

Give Your Best

Finally then, brethren, we urge and exhort in the Lord Jesus that you should abound more and more, just as you received from us how you ought to walk and to please God; for you know what commandments we gave you through the Lord Jesus.

(1 THESSALONIANS 4:1-2)

When Henry Kissinger was Secretary of State of the United States, an aide in the White House approached him with a report. Kissinger asked, 'Is this the best you can do?' The aide sheepishly replied that he could do better. A few days later, the aide returned and resubmitted his work. Kissinger inquired again, 'Is this the best you can do?' The aide reluctantly admitted he could do better. This interaction went on several more times until finally the White House aide responded, 'Yes, it is the best I can do!' Henry Kissinger took the report and said, 'Now, I will read it.'

I guess this story would remind each one of us that there is always room for improvement. There are so many areas of our lives in which we could do better. Our best is yet to be given. This is true in general, and particularly true in relation to our relationship with God. Which one of us would argue with the reality that our knowledge of God could be deeper, our prayers to God bolder, our work for God greater, and our desires for God stronger?

In 1 Thessalonians 4:1-2, Paul urges the Thessalonians to go the second mile spiritually. Paul urges them to acquire a holy distaste for mediocrity. There can be no sitting back in smug satisfaction. Their track record was good, but it could be better. They could improve on what they were already doing. He wants them to abound more and more in the things of God (1 Thess. 3:12; 2 Thess. 1:3). The word translated 'abound' carries the idea of excelling, of exceeding boundaries. It speaks of being over the top. Paul's point is that Christ ought never to be the Lord of the leftovers. The Lord Jesus Christ deserves and demands our very best every time and in everything (Eccles. 9:10; 1 Cor. 10:31). As we abide in Him and His Word in us we can bear fruit, more fruit, and much fruit (John 15:1-10). The language of the New Testament Christian life is that of overflowing and abundance (John 10:10; Rom. 15:13; 2 Cor. 8:2). We can do better than our best in Christ. Our best is yet to be given (Phil. 3:12-16).

This exhortation to do more and be more comes through Paul by the authority of Jesus Christ (1 Thess. 4:1-2). Christ commands it, Christ enables it, and Christ deserves it. Christ deserves our best because everything about His love for us and His work for us on Calvary is over the top. There is nothing measured or comparative about what God has done for us in the Lord Jesus. Think about the *exceeding* riches of His grace toward us (Eph. 2:7). Think about the grace, faith, and love *poured* out on us (1 Tim. 1:14). Think about the *exceeding* greatness of His power toward us (Eph. 1:19). Think about the *exceeding* weight of glory that awaits us (2 Cor. 4:7). Think about the ability of God to do '*exceedingly abundantly* above all that we can ask or think' (Eph. 3:20). He is truly an exceptional God who loves to do exceedingly great things!

'Love divine, all loves excelling,' as the old hymn goes. In the gospel we have heaven's best given freely and fully for earth's worst. Let us therefore give our best in the light of God's best.

Give your best today!

God, Your love is better than life. (Ps. 63:3),
so help me give my life for Your love.
In Jesus' Name, amen.

Risking It All

For indeed he was sick almost unto death; but God had mercy on him, and not only on him but on me also, lest I should have sorrow upon sorrow.

(PHILIPPIANS 2:27)

Before there was Federal Express, there was the Pony Express. The Pony Express was a private express company that carried mail, $2.50 an ounce, by an organized relay of horseback riders. The eastern end was in St. Joseph, Missouri, and the western terminal was in Sacramento, California. If the weather cooperated and danger was averted, a piece of mail would complete the entire two-thousand-mile journey in a nifty ten days. That involved the riders covering seventy-five to a hundred miles a day, while changing horses every fifteen to twenty-five miles. It was clearly not a job for the fainthearted. In fact, one might wonder how they marketed for this dangerous job? An 1860 San Francisco newspaper printed this ad for the Pony Express: 'WANTED: Young, skinny, wiry fellows, not over eighteen. Must be expert riders willing to risk daily. Orphans preferred.' Amazingly, the Pony Express never had a shortage of riders.[1]

Like the Pony Express, serving God through spreading the gospel is not a job for the casually interested. It is a costly business. Fulfilling the Great Commission and living the Great Commandment makes demands and involves risks (Matt. 28:18-20; 22:36-40). The gospel message of a Savior who died cannot be shared or spread powerfully by those who want to keep their lives (Matt. 16:25)! Risking it all for the sake of Christ and those without Christ was the hallmark of early Christianity (Acts 15:26; Rom. 16:4). For those early Christians, coming to the cross of Christ for salvation meant coming away with a cross (Luke 9:23). Theirs was not a religion in which Jesus did all the dying.

We see this disregard for life and limb for the sake of Christ fleshed out memorably and marvelously in the life of

---

1. Donald S. Whitney, *Spiritual Disciplines of the Christian Life* (Colorado Springs, CO: Navpress, 1991), p. 109.

Epaphroditus (Phil. 2:25-30). In writing to the Philippians, Paul commends the gallantry of this selfless servant of Christ who came close to dying while seeking to bring a gift from the Philippians to Paul (Phil. 2:30). Epaphroditus put his life on the line to fulfill the desire of the Philippians to meet Paul's needs in prison. He literally gambled with his life for the sake of Paul's life. When Paul talks about him 'not regarding his life', he is using a word that speaks of gambling, of rolling the dice, of risking it all. It was a word that was used of those who nursed the seriously sick and buried the dead. It was a word that was used of merchants that chanced death for the sake of material gain. It was a word that was used of those who risked their lives in advocating for a friend before the emperor. Epaphroditus was God's gambler.

What are you and I risking for the souls of men, the good of the church, and the glory of God? Playing it safe is death to God's work in our lives. Like the turtle, we can only make progress when we stick our necks out.

God, You gave Your life for me, so help me take risks for You.
In Jesus' Name, amen.

It's My Pleasure

*By faith Enoch was taken away so that he did not see death,
'and was not found, because God had taken him'; for before
he was taken he had this testimony, that he pleased God.*

(HEBREWS 11:5)

David Brainerd was a young man with a contagious love for
God in a world without love for God. In the early eighteenth
century, he dedicated himself to missionary work among the
American Indians of New England. He is famous for the journal
he kept of his life in God and his longings for God. Across the
years this journal has fueled many a life on fire for God. Brainerd
did not live a long life, but he did live a full life. Tuberculosis
shortened his life, and two weeks before his death at the tender
age of twenty-nine, he called his friends to his bedside. His
dying words reveal the passion of his life! He said, 'My heaven
is to please God, and glorify Him, and give all to Him, and to be
wholly devoted to His glory. That is the heaven I long for; that
is my religion, and that is my happiness ... I do not go to heaven
to be advanced, but to give honor to God ... All my desire is to
glorify God ... I see nothing else in the world than can yield any
satisfaction besides living to God, pleasing Him, and doing His
will.'[2]

David Brainerd's greatest pleasure while on earth was to
please the God of heaven. That was his heaven before he was
even in heaven! It was his dying testimony that he found his joy
in delighting the heart of God. Interestingly, the Bible points
to another man who had that very same testimony. According
to the writer to the Hebrews, Enoch was a man who 'had this
testimony, that he pleased God' (Heb. 11:5). God's Word tells us
that Enoch lived in the seventh generation from Adam, between
the fall and the flood, which was a period marked by the spread
of sin ending in death (Gen. 5:1-32; Rom. 5:12). Ironically, Enoch's
testimony of pleasing God is placed in the midst of the reign
of death, although Enoch himself would not die (Gen. 5:21-4).

---

2. Gary Inrig, *A Call to Excellence* (Wheaton, IL: Victor Books, 1985),
p. 57.

This was a period leading up to the days of Noah (Gen. 6:1-8). These were days marked by a rising tide of evil, days that would trigger the judgment of the flood. In living for God, Enoch cut against the grain of the culture. Like David Brainerd, Enoch's heaven was to please God. This was so much the case that one day while walking with God, he walked straight into heaven (Gen. 5:24; Heb. 11:5). Enoch's communion with God was so real that the transition from earth to heaven was seamless. The move to heaven required very little adjustment.

In a world where men love to please themselves and pursue pleasure apart from God, may we follow in the footsteps of Enoch, a man who walked with God, a man who had this testimony that he pleased God. May we make it our aim to be found pleasing to God when we make the transition from earth to heaven (2 Cor. 5:9-11)! Some of the ways we can do that is (1) by displaying faith in God (Heb. 11:6); (2) by being spiritually minded (Rom. 8:6-8); (3) by fearing God (Ps. 147:11); (4) by exalting and following Christ (Matt. 17:5); (5) by complete obedience to God's Word (1 Sam. 15:22-3); (6) by doing God's will (Heb. 13:22); and (7) by being generous in our praise toward God for his many blessings (Heb. 13:15-16). As those created for His pleasure, may our greatest joy be found in bringing joy and pleasure to God (Col. 1:16-17; Rev. 4:11; Phil. 2:13). God did not put us on the earth to please ourselves, but to please Him, which is pure joy (Pss. 16:11; 37:4)!

God, pursuing You is genuine joy. Remind me that it is
a pleasure and privilege to please You.
In Jesus' Name, amen.

Familiarity Breeds Contempt

And many hearing Him were astonished, saying, 'Where did this Man get these things? And what wisdom is this which is given to Him, that such mighty works are performed by His hands! Is this not the carpenter, the Son of Mary, and brother of James, Joses, Judas, and Simon? And are not His sisters here with us?' So they were offended at Him.

(MARK 6:2-3)

Author and pastor Max Lucado tells of a time when he almost lost his two-year-old daughter. A parent's worst nightmare became real life when his little girl accidentally fell into a swimming pool one day. Although a tragedy was averted, Lucado admits that on his part there had been carelessness and a taking for granted attitude that led to almost losing her. In his book, *God Came Near*, he reflects:

> I came face to face with one of the underground's slyest agents, the agent of familiarity. His commission from the black throne is clear and fatal. Take nothing from your victim; cause him only to take everything for granted. He (familiarity) had been on my trail for years and I never knew it. But I know it now. I've come to recognize his talents and detect his presence. And I am doing my best to keep him out. His aim is deadly. His goal is nothing less than to take what is most precious to us, and make it appear common.

Familiarity breeding contempt, or taking things and people for granted, is a clear and present danger. Lives are put in jeopardy because we underestimate familiarity's threat. Marriages run aground because its menace is ignored. A spirit of gratitude is often absent because it is present. We become lazy in worship because it is work. As Max Lucado warns, taking things, people, and God for granted is a work of the enemy. That is why we must work harder at giving thanks for everything, jealously guarding love, prizing people, seeing the big in the small, and worshiping God as our chief joy. We must fear the dawning of a day in life when everything becomes common and we lose our capacity to wonder.

The danger of familiarity breeding contempt is sadly on display in Jesus' rejection by the people of Nazareth (Mark 6:1-6). This was His hometown, and yet the people that should have known Jesus best understood Him the least. He was a prophet without honor in his own town (Mark 4:4). There was skepticism, even cynicism about Jesus. They reasoned that Jesus was a carpenter who builds tables, but doesn't do miracles. He is Mary's son, not God's son (4:2-3). For them, the glory of Christ's person and work was hidden behind a veil of ordinariness. Paradoxically, they didn't marvel at Him; rather He marveled at them because of their unbelief (4:5-6). Instead of being lost in wonder, love, and praise toward Christ, they were offended by Him (6:3). Christ was a scandal in the town. Familiarity had bred contempt. Those who had lived in proximity to Christ were far from appreciating or understanding Him.

To a lesser extent, that can even happen after faith in Christ. The pearl of great price, Jesus Himself, can lose His luster (Matt. 13:45-6). We can lose our taste for the goodness of God. We can lose our first love. The things of God can become humdrum. We no longer shiver at the thought of hell and no longer smile at the thought of heaven. We no longer fawn at the thought of Christ. We have sadly and scarily begun to neglect and take for granted so great a salvation and Savior (Heb. 2:3). Today, fight that work of the enemy in your soul that would take what is most precious, the gospel and Christ, and make it appear common.

'To you who believe, He is precious' (1 Pet. 2:7).

God, You are extraordinary, so guard my heart against treating
You as ordinary.
In Jesus' Name, amen.

Surviving
the Struggle to Keep My Priorities Straight

The First Place

All things were created through Him and for Him. And He is before all things, and in Him all things consist. And He is the head of the body, the church, who is the beginning, the firstborn from the dead, that in all things He may have the preeminence.

(COLOSSIANS 1:16-18)

Gandhi was a great admirer of Christ. He considered the life of Christ a beautiful example of the perfect man. He was deeply impressed by Christ's teaching in the Sermon on the Mount and sought to follow its message. He viewed Christ as the embodiment of sacrifice and a great example to the world. But he would not go any further than that, and remained a Hindu throughout his life.

Someone once asked him, 'Mr Gandhi, though you quote the words of the Christ often, why is it that you appear so adamantly to reject becoming His follower?' Gandhi replied, 'Oh, I don't reject your Christ. I like your Christ. I don't like your Christians. Your Christians are so unlike your Christ.' When Gandhi was killed in 1948, among his few material possessions and belongings were about a dozen books, including the *Life and Teachings of Jesus Christ* and the Gospel of John. On the wall by his side was a portrait of Jesus with these words, 'He is our peace.' Christ had evidently found a place within the circumference of his life, but never its center. In fact, Gandhi summarized his position on Jesus when he said, 'I cannot concede to Christ a solitary throne.'

There are many people like Gandhi who are willing to give Christ a place in their lives, but not a solitary throne. They will have Jesus, the son of Mary, but not Jesus, the Son of God (Matt. 3:17). They will have Jesus, the teacher, but not Jesus, the eternal Word (John 1:1). They will have Jesus, the martyr, but not Christ, the redeemer, dying for the sins of the world (1 John 2:2). For such people, Christ is to be admired, but not worshipped, viewed as special but not supreme.

In his letter to the Colossians, Paul deals with this reductionist view of Christ. The church at Colossae was being infected and infiltrated by an early form of Gnosticism which taught that Jesus was only one of thousands of emanations from God, that He was a disembodied spiritual being created by God, that He was only a rung on the ladder towards God. Paul writes to confront such thinking and to establish the sufficiency and supremacy of Christ over creation and within the church. In a crash course on Christology, Paul shows that Christ was the full resemblance of God in bodily form, ranked above all of creation, the sustainer and sovereign of all created things, the head of the church, the genesis of history, and the conqueror of death (Col. 1:15-18). Christ is not penultimate; He is ultimate. He takes second place to no one or nothing. Christ must therefore be afforded the first place and a solitary throne (Col. 1:18; 3:11).

As Christians, Jesus' lordship is part of our creed, but is it part of our conduct? When it comes to our lives, is Christ in the back seat, passenger seat, or driver's seat? Jesus was never meant to be a back seat driver.

God, You are the King of kings and Lord of lords (1 Tim. 6:15),
so let me honor You as such!
In Jesus' Name, amen.

First Things First

And though I bestow all my goods to feed the poor, and though I give my body to be burned, but have not love, it profits me nothing.

(1 CORINTHIANS 13:3)

Coach Bobby Bowden of Florida State liked to inspire his teams with parables. According to Tennessee Titans' center Kevin Long, who played under Bowden, one of Bowden's favorite stories centered on his playing days in college baseball. Bowden had never hit a home run until one day he hit one down the right-field line, into the corner. Seizing the opportunity, he rounds first, and glances over to the third-base coach. He turned at second, was halfway to third, and the coach was still waving him on. Coming down the stretch with the focus and force of an Olympic sprinter, Bowden hits home plate. He had his first home run. There were high fives all round from his fellow teammates. But in the midst of the celebrations, the pitcher took the ball, threw it to the first baseman, and the umpire called him out. Retelling the story Coach Bowden reminds his players: 'If you don't take care of first base, it doesn't matter what you do.'[1]

As this story reminds us, some things must be done first before other things can be done at all. In life as in baseball, first base first, is an important principle. Some things give substance, significance, and success to everything else. Love patterned after Christ is one of those things. According to Paul in First Corinthians 13, love for God and others is a first base thing in the Christian life (1 Cor. 13:1-3). Without it nothing else really matters. To make his point, Paul stretches a point. Paul wants us to imagine a man who has the tongue of an orator, the mind of a scholar, the spirit of a pioneer, and the heart of a martyr. Imagine a man who is John Chrysostom, Jonathan Edwards, George Mueller, and Jim Elliott rolled into one, a 'spiritual superman' we might say. Yet, Paul tells us that this man and his ministry apart from the practice of love is a big fat

---

1. PreachingToday.com, *More Perfect Illustrations*, (Wheaton, IL: Tyndale House Publishers, 2003) pp. 219-20.

zero. Without love gilding everything he does, he is nothing and achieves nothing.

According to the Bible, love patterned after Jesus Christ – unwarranted, costly, selfless, and enduring love – is central to all that we are and do. To love is to live; to love not is to live not (1 John 3:14). Love must define our being and direct our doing. Why? First, God is love (1 John 4:8, 16). Love is not a quality God possesses; it is the essence of His being. He demonstrates it in a myriad of ways, most of all, on the cross (Rom. 5:8). Second, love for God is the first and greatest commandment (Mark 12:28-34). The sum and summit of Christian duty is love for God. Third, love for others is the touchstone of Christian discipleship (John 13:34-5). Fourth, love is the crowning virtue of Christian character (Gal. 5:22). Love is the queen of all Christian graces. Peace is love at rest. Goodness is love in action. Temperance is love in harness. Skevington Wood writes: 'Where love is present it matters not what is absent, where love is absent it matters not what is present' (Prov. 15:17). Before you take one more step today, why not stop and make sure that you are taking care of this first base in the Christian life!

God, Your love is supreme!
Help love to reign supreme in my life as well.
In Jesus' Name, amen.

Setting Priorities

And Jesus answered and said to her, 'Martha, Martha, you are worried and troubled about many things. But one thing is needed, and Mary has chosen that good part, which will not be taken away from her.'

(LUKE 10:41-2)

Filmmaker Walt Disney was known for chopping anything from his movies that got in the way of the story's progress and pace. Ward Kimball can attest to that fact! Ward Kimball, one of the animators for *Snow White*, recalls working 240 days on a 4½ minute sequence in which the dwarfs made soup for Snow White and almost destroyed the kitchen in the process. Walt Disney thought it funny, but he also thought it disrupted the flow of the film, and so he cut it from the picture. In the editing room of Disney Studios, the question was never 'Is it good?' but 'Is it best?' Snow White was not a good movie; it was a great movie. Why? Because Walt Disney set priorities and kept to them.[2]

In the light of this story, we would want life to imitate art. In life, we must make it our mission to stay on mission, which means setting priorities. It is easy to get drawn away from those things that should command our greatest attention and affection. An example of what we are talking about is to be found in Luke's Gospel, where we read of Jesus' visit to the home of Mary and Martha (Luke 10:38-42). Upon welcoming Jesus into her home, Martha immediately sets about fixing the Lord Jesus something to eat and becomes 'distracted with much serving' (10:40). Her sister Mary makes a different choice. She sits at Jesus feet and hears His word (10:39). She seeks fellowship with the Bread of Life Himself (John 6:35). Mary's unwillingness to help in the kitchen bothers Martha, and so she makes a stink about it (Luke 10:40). Martha doesn't like Mary's choice. Interestingly, Jesus tells Martha that he liked Mary's choice. Mary had understood that 'man shall not live by bread alone, but by every word that proceeds from the mouth of God'

---

2. Steve J. Lawson, *The Legacy* (Sisters, OR: Multnomah Publishers, 1998), p. 28.

(Matt. 4:4). According to Jesus, Mary had given herself to that which was most needful, that which was best, and that which would have a lasting impact on her life (Luke 10:42). She did not allow the pressing to crowd out the needful, the good to crowd out the best, and the temporal to crowd out the eternal. She made a choice based on what was needful, best, and lasting.

Question! When the film of our lives is shown before the face of God and the hosts of heaven, will it be as great as it might be? The answer to that question will depend on the editing we do during our days on earth. Some things in life are to be desired, pursued, and valued more than other things (Ps. 27:4; Phil. 3:13; Luke 10:41-2). Will we, like Walt Disney, ruthlessly cut away anything that disrupts the unfolding of God's story in us and through us? Like Mary, we must not allow the pressing to crowd out the necessary, the good to crowd out the best, and the temporal to crowd out the eternal! Make it your mission to stay on mission. Learn to distinguish between what really ought to matter, and what is mattering.

God, You are my greatest necessity!
Assist me in setting right priorities for the right reasons.
In Jesus' Name, amen.

Learn to Say No

Now in the morning, having risen a long while before daylight, He went out and departed to a solitary place and there He prayed.

(MARK 1:35)

A man unpacked his lunch in the factory cafeteria, and complained to his fellow worker, 'I don't believe it, bologna again! This is the fourth straight day I have had this!' His fellow worker responded, 'Well, why don't you tell your wife you're tired of bologna?' 'You don't understand,' the man said. 'I'm single. I pack my own lunches.'

We laugh, but the joke is on us. We complain about our schedule being too full, but the truth is we packed much of it ourselves. We find it hard to say no to good opportunities, and good causes. We find it hard to strike a balance between work, rest, and play. We find it hard to distinguish between what God wants us to do and what others think we should be doing. As parents, as employees or employers, as servants of God, and as members of society, we think we should be doing it all. We try to divide ourselves equally among all these things until there is nothing left of us. Our busyness has led to barrenness. Our families are fractured, our walk with God lifeless, our relationships with friends and neighbors are shallow, and our health is taking a hit. The fact is that a book without margins is unreadable, and a life without margins is unlivable.

We need to create margins, and that begins by learning to say no. We have got to slow down the snowball effect of doing more things with less time and energy. But saying yes to saying no is not easy for us. After all, time is short, eternity is long, and the needs are great. All those things are true, but it is also true that we can end up doing a lot of things that are not wrong in themselves, but they are just not right for us, and it would be wrong to give time to them. Remember, if the devil cannot make us bad he will make us busy. We have got to learn to say no.

Let me give you several incentives in learning to say no:

First, learn to say no because Jesus did. Jesus didn't meet every need (Mark 1:35-9). People went unhealed. He left one town to preach in another. He spent thirty years in training and only three in ministry. He did not try to do it all. But He did finish the work the Father gave Him to do (John 17:4). Second, learn to say no because redeeming the time is not the same as doing more. Redeeming the time is all about learning what the will of God is for our lives, and doing it (Eph. 5:15-17). Redeeming the time is about what we do, not how much we do. Doing one more thing is not the same as living wisely. Third, learn to say no because we all have different gifts and callings (1 Cor. 12:12-31; 1 Pet. 4:10-11). Each person is like a perfectly formed jigsaw piece within God's plan. Our individual roles are unique, not universal. God hasn't called us to do it all, He has called us to do certain things alongside others who are doing other things. Spurgeon said, 'Learn to say no, it will be of more use to you than being able to read Latin.'

God, thank You for gifting me in specific ways.
Help me to find those ways and live on point with purpose.
In Jesus' Name, amen.

No Time to Waste

See then that you walk circumspectly, not as fools but as wise, redeeming the time, because the days are evil. Therefore do not be unwise, but understand what the will of the Lord is.

(EPHESIANS 5:15-17)

Thomas Chalmers was a minister in the Church of Scotland, who in the early days of his pastorate did not know God. He was not known for his godliness. Not known to God, not known for his godliness, but he was well known for a notorious comment he made in 1805 about the Christian ministry. He said, 'After the satisfactory discharge of his parish duties, a minister may enjoy five days of uninterrupted leisure, for the prosecution of any science in which his taste may dispose him to engage.' He was a man without a passion for God, and a distinctly low view of the ministry. But all that changed when God got his attention through a broken engagement, serious illness, and the death of his sister and two brothers to tuberculosis. Thomas Chalmers's life was turned upside down, and his theories inside out. By 1811, he was a new man with a new ministry. Gone were the lazy and hazy days of his earlier ministry. As a truly converted man and minister, he set about making Christ, His gospel, and His church his all-consuming pursuit. His newfound evangelical fervor was a distinct contrast to his earlier years. So much so that in 1825 an opponent of Chalmers within the Church of Scotland cited his own words of 1805. Chalmers repudiated his past conviction with these words: 'I had forgotten two magnitudes: I thought not of the littleness of time, and I recklessly thought not of the greatness of eternity.'

How easy it is to forget these two great magnitudes: the brevity of time and the endlessness of eternity. To forget that we will not live forever, and yet we will live forever, that this life is the dressing room for the next. Thomas Chalmers realized, and so must we, that there is no time to waste. Time is of the essence, life is short, and eternity is long (Pss. 39:4-6; 90:12). That is why we must take deliberate steps to ensure that our lives are lived for the glory of God, and within His will (Eph. 5:15-17).

In Ephesians 5:15, Paul tells the Christians at Ephesus to walk circumspectly, not as fools, but as wise. They are not to dither or dilly-dally. The idea lying behind the word 'circumspectly' is that of choosing carefully. Louis Talbot in his commentary on Ephesians writes: 'Circumspectly means "to pick the way," to be careful how we walk, as though we were walking on ground filled with broken bottles.' It is the thought of carefully choosing your next step within the will of God. Life is serious business given the shortness of time and the length of eternity. Therefore, we must determine every day to give our hearts to God, our minds to meditate on His Word, our mouths to sing His praise, our hands to serve humanity, and our feet to walk the paths of righteousness. This must be our priority and passion.

That is why Paul urges the Ephesians to buy up every opportunity within life to do the will of God (Eph. 5:16-17). To 'redeem the time' is not an issue of time management. It is not about doing more things, but about doing the right things (Matt. 6:33). It is about understanding what the will of God is in a given situation, and doing it (1 John 2:15-17). The day must be seized for God's glory. There is no time to waste. Redeeming the time is not simply about being busy, but about being smart. As my mother used to say to our family, 'Only one life to live will soon be past, only what's done for Jesus will last.'

God, thank You for the gift of time.
Help me to be responsible and redemptive with the life
You give me.
In Jesus' Name, amen.

Make it Your Habit

As for me, I will call upon God, and the LORD shall save me. Evening and morning and at noon I will pray, and cry aloud, and He shall hear my voice. He has redeemed my soul in peace from the battle that was against me, for there were many against me.

(PSALM 55:16-18)

The story is told of an old European monastery that sat on the edge of a high cliff. It was accessible only by a terrifying ride in a swaying basket. Brave-hearted visitors to the monastery were hoisted up in the basket by a single rope and a series of pulleys. One particular visitor noticed on the ride up that the rope was rather old and frayed at certain parts. Hoping to quell his anxiety, he asked the monk riding in the basket with him, 'How often do you change the rope?' The monk nonchalantly replied, 'Whenever it breaks!' Yikes!

Waiting for something to break before you fix it is a bad policy in life. Good sense tells us that machinery requires constant maintenance. Likewise relationships need to be kept in good repair. And when it comes to our spiritual life, good habits need to be practiced as well.

In terms of our walk with God, spontaneity is overrated. Routine and repetition are spiritual lifesavers. Spiritual depth is never last minute. Why? Because we become what we repeatedly do. Spiritual excellence and effectiveness is not an act; it is a habit. For example, if prayer is to be a powerful force in our lives, it must not be the exception, but the prevailing posture and attitude of our daily lives. In light of our opening story, we must not wait for the rope to snap before we pray or before we begin to learn how to pray. For prayer to be a spiritual dynamic in our lives, it must first be a spiritual discipline. The Bible says that prayer is to be a habit in our lives, not an act (Eph. 6:18; 1 Thess. 5:17). If the Christian is to find God's help through prayer, then life and its challenging moments need to find the Christian in prayer and at prayer regularly.

In Psalm 55 David exemplifies this ideal of creating greater routine and regularity in our prayer lives. He makes prayer a habit, not an act. King David needed to pray for God's help because he was in a fight for his life amidst Absalom's rebellion and Ahithophel's treachery (Ps. 55:9-14; cp. 2 Sam. 15:37; 16:20–17:23). But David does pray, and according to the text, the king prayed three times a day: evening, morning, and noon (Ps. 55:17). These set times of prayer for the faithful Jew can also be seen in the life of Daniel (Dan. 6:10). David, like Daniel, had customary times of prayer. There was a regiment and a rhythm to his spiritual life. The point not to be missed is that trouble found David at prayer and had trouble defeating him. Although David was tempted to run, he was enabled to stand (Pss. 55:6-8; 22). The discipline of visiting the secret place to pray three times a day was David's secret. David knew how to pray when he needed to pray the most. His prayer life was not haphazard or simply spontaneous! The king knew his way to the throne of grace; the path was well worn and his knees were flexible. It is no surprise then that David kept his balance amidst this tempest of hatred because his appointed times of prayer before God acted as a counterbalance.

The point! Good spiritual habits help us survive the bad days. Rarely do we get our spiritual act together in the midst of disjointed circumstances and spinning emotions.

Be in the habit of praying when life calls for greater prayer!

God, prayer is vital at all times.
Help me to get in the habit.
In Jesus' Name, amen.

Surviving
the Struggle to Know
What to do Next

Spoiled for Choice

For this is God, Our God forever and ever; He will be our guide even to death.

(PSALM 48:14)

Daniel Boone was one of the heroes of the American frontier. It is said that he was once returning from the uncharted forests beyond the Kentucky River and was asked by a lady if he had ever been lost. The famous scout replied, 'I cannot say I was ever lost, ma'am, but I was bewildered for three days.'

Life can indeed be a bewildering experience as we work our way through a forest of decisions that line up one after another. Life was not a choice for anyone of us, but living life is full of choices. One study conducted several years ago by the University of Minnesota discovered that we all face between 300 and 17,000 decisions every day. On any given day these choices might range from making travel plans, to the switching off of a life support machine that is sustaining the existence of a loved one. Sooner or later all of us arrive at junctures where two roads diverge.

What are we to do when we come to a fork in the road of life? The good news is that God has not left us simply to lean on our own understanding, but is willing to act as our guide in life and even unto death (Ps. 48:14; Prov. 3:5-6).

Here are several angles to God's guidance that help us to take a step in the right direction:

* Read and heed the Scriptures (Ps. 119:105; 2 Tim. 3:16-17). God has graciously revealed His mind and will in the corpus of the sixty-six books of the Bible and they can equip us sufficiently unto every good work. The precepts and principles of God's Word act as a light unto our path!

* Think with a renewed mind (Rom. 12:1-2; 2 Tim. 2:7). The Lord gave us a lot of leading when he gave us a brain, and when our thinking is submitted to God's thinking we can often reason our way to an answer within His will.

* Pray humbly (James 1:5). According to James, God is a treasure trove of wisdom, and prayer is the key to unlocking

that wisdom. But if that key is to work, it must be found in the hand of the humble soul who prays for God's will to be done on earth, not man's will to reign in heaven (Matt. 6:9-10). Remember, prayer is not so much us telling God what we want but us asking God what He wants.

* Seek the counsel and example of godly people (Prov. 11:14; 1 Thess. 1:6). Life is a team sport, and so we need the coaching of others. We need the objective, wise, and godly counsel of parents, pastors, and peers.

God, Your way is best. Guide me in making the right decisions in a world spoilt by choice.
In Jesus' Name, amen.

That's An Easy Decision

Therefore, whether you eat or drink, or whatever you do, do all to the glory of God.

(1 CORINTHIANS 10:31)

A young man came to the late Bible teacher J. Vernon McGee and said, 'Dr McGee, I have been studying predestination, and I am so convinced of the sovereignty of God that I believe if I stood in the middle of a busy highway, and my hour was not yet come, God would and could spare my life.' Dr McGee, responding with his characteristic wit, said, 'Son, if you stand in the middle of a busy highway, your hour has come.'

God's sovereignty over our lives does not cancel out our responsibility to exercise good judgment in our decisions. Decisions that rush at us like oncoming traffic! How do we exercise good judgment in our decisions? Not every decision in life is easy, but it can be made easier by following a series of principles that Paul outlines in his first letter to the Corinthians. In 1 Corinthians 8–10 especially, we find Paul instructing the Corinthians how to make decisions in matters of conscience where there is no clear prohibition or permission from the Lord. The principles he teaches are applicable to many situations and help make the hard decisions easy. Here is some advice to affect your decisions:

EXPEDIENCE: Will it be spiritually beneficial (1 Cor. 6:12; 10:23)? There are many things the Christian can do that are not wrong, but are they spiritually enriching? Are they the best use of our time? Are they the best use of our powers and gifts?

EDIFICATION: Will it build me up (1 Cor. 10:23; 14:26)? Before taking to a certain path in life, we need to be sure that it will not work against our faith in Christ. Whatever we add to our lives must not subtract from our faith and its stability and strength.

EXAMPLE: Will it help or hinder other Christians (1 Cor. 8:9-13)? Any choice we make must bear others in mind. Our freedoms were not given to make us autonomous.

We are given liberty in Christ in order to be the servants of others, not in order to indulge our own preferences. We must therefore be self-limiting in our choices.

ENSLAVEMENT: Will this pursuit control me (1 Cor. 6:12)? Given Christ's unrivaled lordship over our lives and our own calling to be rulers over the earth, we must not be mastered by anything in any choice that we make. Our choices must not be allowed to make a prisoner out of us.

EXALTATION: Will this activity glorify our glorious God (1 Cor. 10:31)? Man's sole purpose is to glorify God. Therefore we have no better choice but to do that which best glorifies God.

God, thank You that You have given us principles to help us make decisions.
Help my decisions most of all to exalt You and edify others and myself.
In Jesus' Name, amen.

Taking the Next Step

... the waters which came down from upstream stood still, and rose in a heap very far away at Adam, the city that is beside Zaretan. So the waters that went down into the Sea of the Arabah, the Salt Sea, failed, and were cut off; and the people crossed over opposite Jericho.

(JOSHUA 3:16)

What is stopping you from taking that next step? What is holding you back from boldly moving forward? Is it the size of the task? Is it the doubts of friends and family? Is it the fear of failure? Is it the security of the familiar? There you stand on the doorstep of a great opportunity brilliantly disguised as an impossible situation.

This was the situation of the children of Israel on the edge of entering the Promised Land. In Joshua chapter 3, the Israelites are looking across to Canaan with the Jordan River at flood level standing in their way (Josh. 3:1-17). The river's edge was becoming a swamp (3:15). It seems that God had brought them to the east bank of the Jordan River at a most unpropitious time. The more they looked, the more impossible the crossing seemed. No boats, no bridges, no way!

Faced with this improbable and impossible situation, God tells the Israelites to take a step of faith by following the priests who bear the Ark of the Covenant into the river (Josh. 3:11-13). God promises them that if they will march forward by faith in obedience to Him, He will dam up the Jordan River as soon as their feet touch the water, enabling them to cross. This is not unlike the Red Sea episode (3:13-16; cp. Exod. 14:15-16). Trusting God, they did take that next step towards Canaan. Passing through the waters, God proved that He was with them and for them in a most marvelous way (Isa. 43:2).

Got any rivers you think cannot be crossed? Well, this story teaches us that there are no God-sized solutions until we get our feet wet in boldly and believingly taking the next step toward what we know to be the will of God for us. Heaven moves to help when we step out in faith to obey. We must look to the Lord (Josh. 3:11). We must also sanctify ourselves in prayerful preparation (3:5). But those things are not enough, for we must also be willing to get our feet wet in bold action (3:13). If we are going to do anything for God and God for us, we must take that first step into the swelling tide, showing our faith to be large and our God to be big. Without faith, it is impossible to please God, and without God, things remain impossible (Heb. 11:6).

In 1994, June and I decided to pack up and leave Northern Ireland with our three young daughters so I could attend The Master's Seminary in Southern California. It was a big and bold move. But God encouraged us with a paraphrase of the words in Proverbs 4:12: 'As you go, the way shall open up to you.' As a trustee of that school today, God has proved that promise to us in an unbelievable way. But it all started with a step of faith. Go get your feet wet!

God, thank You that You accompany me on my journey.
Encourage me to get my feet wet.
In Jesus' Name, amen.

Making Plans

For what is your life? It is even a vapor that appears for a little time and then vanishes away. Instead you ought to say, 'If the Lord wills, we shall live and do this or that.' But now you boast in your arrogance. All such boasting is evil.
(JAMES 4:14-16)

At the age of sixty-seven, John Chancellor was just easing his way into retirement after forty-three years as a journalist. He was seen often on the NBC Nightly News. At this point in his life, there was not a cloud in the sky. All was well and life was good. Then he discovered he had stomach cancer. At first he was angry and fought with God. In time, however, he came to terms with his situation and made peace with God. Just before his death, he made this statement, 'If you want to make God laugh, tell Him your plans.'

What an honest, humble, and even humorous statement – one that we would do well to reflect upon as we make our plans for the next thing in life. Sometimes our talk of the future is marked by an arrogant boasting. In pride, we presume we are the masters of our own fate. We forget that God alone is sovereign, life is His gift, and He governs it all (Acts 17:28; Rom. 11:33). Our plans ought therefore to be drawn in pencil and made subject to a sovereign God who works all things according to the counsel of His own will (Prov. 16:9; 33:11; Eph. 1:11).

Interestingly, this is the counsel that the apostle James gives to a group of businessmen who were drawing up a plan of attack for the next year (James 4:13-17). James takes them to task, not for their planning which seems prudent, but for their presumptiveness and prayerlessness, which failed to acknowledge God's control over life. In all their planning there was no praying. They had failed to say, 'If the Lord wills, we shall live and do this and that' (4:15). These professing Christians were acting in their business lives as practical atheists. They were boasting about a tomorrow they may not see, for life is but a vapor that appears for a little time (4:14; Prov. 27:1). James wants to see from them a greater humility before God, and recognition of the fact that success comes from Him (4:10; Ps. 75:6-7).

We would all do well to remember what Napoleon forgot, 'Man proposes but God disposes.' In light of the fact that God deals the cards and holds all the aces, it would be prudent of us to do three things. First, we ought to prayerfully acknowledge God in all our ways (Prov. 3:5-6). Second, we ought to be flexible about our plans, making them subject to divine approval and alterations (Rom. 1:10; 1 Cor. 16:7). And finally, we ought to live life to the fullest today (Ps. 118:24; Eccles. 9:9-12).

In planning for an uncertain future, don't forget to make the most of today. Live to the full every situation you believe to be the will of God. Don't make yourself cry and God laugh over plans that you never made subject to His will. Above all, plan to live His plan (Eph. 2:10)!

God, You reign over all, so help me to trust every tomorrow
to You.
In Jesus' Name, amen.

Leaving a Legacy

So all the days of Enoch were three hundred and sixty-five years. And Enoch walked with God; and he was not, for God took him.

(GENESIS 5:23-4)

In winning the 2015 British Open at St. Andrews, Scotland, PGA golf player Zach Johnson said: 'I feel like God gave me the ability to play a game. I try to take it seriously. I realize it's just a game ... this [win] isn't going to define me or my career, at least I hope it doesn't. It's not my legacy. Granted, as a professional athlete and as a golfer, I'm going to relish this. I'm going to savor this. I'm humbled by this. But my legacy should be my kids and family.'

That for me is a hole in one comment! Zach Johnson reminds us that when it comes to life there is no real success without succession. What matters most in life is that we pass on to the next generation what matters most. A legacy of faith in Christ, obedience to Scripture, love for the local church, and concern for the lost and the least is what we urgently need to hand down to our children and our children's children. The Bible says in Proverbs: 'The righteous man walks in his integrity; His children are blessed after him' (Prov. 20:7). While the Bible encourages us to leave a financial legacy to our children, more importantly, it encourages us to leave a spiritual legacy of faith in Christ and the riches of His grace (Prov. 13:22; 19:14; 2 Tim. 1:3-5). Therefore, there is no spiritual success without spiritual succession.

The reality of this is aptly illustrated in the life of the Old Testament character Enoch. In Genesis, Moses tells us that the birth of Enoch's faith in God was triggered by the birth of his son Methuselah (Gen. 5:21-2). Notice that Enoch's walk with God starts with the arrival of his son. It has been well said that God uses both the grave and the cradle to awaken people spiritually. Enoch would not be the last father to sense the nearness and reality of God upon entering fatherhood. Every walk begins with a step, and when Enoch stepped into the role of a parent, it was transformative in that he gave his life to the God who gives life. I think I am right in saying that the ripple effect of this man's faith walk lasted more than 300 years. Consequently, we read that his great grandson Noah also walked with God (Gen. 5:22, 24; 6:9), and became a preacher like his great grandfather (2 Pet. 2:5; Jude 14-15). Enoch did not carve his name on marble, but on the hearts of his children and his children's children. Enoch's walk with God was a wonderful example to his family. The fact that we find Enoch mentioned in a genealogy in Genesis five, not only points to the fact that Genesis is real history, but that we are all links in a family chain and need to live with the idea of leaving a legacy of faith behind us.

What does legacy look like? Here is an acrostic of what leaving a LEGACY involves (1) Love for God and others; (2) Example of godliness; (3) Guidance through Scripture; (4) Availability and presence; (5) Consistency of character; and (6) Yearning for heaven. Our children and family need to see that we are godly in behavior, biblical in thought, real, committed to them, and eternal in our perspective. Money alone is a poor legacy. The real legacy is the treasured memory of faith in God!

God, thank You for using people throughout the generations.
Help me to leave a godly legacy, for that is what lasts.
In Jesus' Name, amen.

Make Your Mind Up and Get on With It

Let each be fully convinced in his own mind.

(ROMANS 14:5)

Sherlock Holmes and Dr Watson went on a camping trip and during the night Holmes said, 'Watson, look up into the sky and tell me what you see.' Watson said, 'I see millions and millions of stars.' Holmes then asked, 'And what does that tell you?' Watson reflected and responded, 'Astronomically, it tells me that there are millions of galaxies, and potentially billions of planets. Theologically, it tells me that God is great, and that we are small. Meteorologically, it tells me that we will have a beautiful day tomorrow.' He then paused for a moment, 'Holmes,' asked Watson, 'What does it tell you?' Holmes retorted, 'It tells me somebody stole our tent.'

Sometimes we can over-analyze a thing and miss the obvious. We can make the simple more complicated than it needs to be. In the Christian life, we often do that when it comes to knowing and doing the will of God. When it comes to general guidance, God expects us to simply make up our mind. The Bible encourages us to use our head and act with prudence. This explains why Paul in Romans informs the saints that it was quite legitimate for them to make up their own minds on disputable matters, so long as their minds were taught by a good conscience (Rom. 14:5). Here the apostle points to a convinced mind being a major factor in guidance. Other New Testament passages point to reason and the use of critical thinking as being part of the godly decision-making process. Thinking terminology like, 'I considered it necessary,' 'it is not desirable,' 'it seemed good,' or simply 'I decided,' is to be found throughout the biblical and apostolic record (Phil. 2:25-6; Acts 6:2-4; 15:28-9; Titus 3:12).

When it comes to guidance, God doesn't just want us to read the Scripture, pray, and seek the advice of others. He wants us to also put our thinking caps on. It is with and through a renewed mind, submitted to the lordship and leadership of Christ, that we can prove what is that good and perfect will of God for us (Rom. 12:1-2). God intends that we more often than not resolve our dilemmas and decisions through clear and critical thinking.

We do this through weighing the options, asking the right questions, and seeking what is reasonable as well as righteous. God generally guides us by presenting reasons to our minds for acting in a certain way.

The Lord gave us a lot of leading when he gave us a brain. If God gave us watches, would we honor Him by asking Him the time of day, or by consulting our timepiece? If God gave the merchant seaman GPS, would the sailor please God more by kneeling to pray for guidance, or by steering the ship according to his satellite navigation system? Except for those things expressly commanded or forbidden in Scripture, God expects us to use our heads. Make up your mind and get on with it.

God, thank You for the gift of my mind.
Help me to use it the way You intend.
In Jesus' Name, amen.

Surviving
the Struggle with Pain
and Suffering

Message in a Bottle

You number my wanderings; Put my tears into Your bottle;
Are they not in Your book?

(PSALM 56:8)

Someone has said that life is a bridge of groans over a river of tears. While that statement may be overly pessimistic, there is nevertheless more than a tinge of realism in it. Life has a way of reducing each of us to a puddle of tears. Which of us has not cried ourselves to sleep or fought back the tears? Ever since the fall of Adam and Eve in the Garden of Eden, we have been eating the bitter fruit of their disobedience. Their disobedience brought sin, and sin brought sorrow, and we have been crying ever since (Gen. 3:16-17; Rom. 8:22-3). That's why it's not a surprise that the Bible is awash with tears. In John 11:35 we find the Lord Jesus crying over the death of Lazarus. In Luke 22:62 we find the apostle Peter weeping bitterly over his denial of Jesus. In Jeremiah 9:1 we find the prophet Jeremiah drowning in tears over the sins of the people of God in Judah. In Acts 20:19 we find Paul humbly serving the Lord with tears. In 2 Samuel 18:33 we find King David crying copiously over his wayward son Absalom. This world is a vale of tears. But to those who are all cried out, I have a wonderful promise from God's Word for you.

In Psalm 56 we find David in a spot of trouble. He has been captured by his mortal enemies the Philistines, and is under lock and key in Gath (1 Sam. 21:10-11). In the midst of these terrifying circumstances, David is seized with a sense of fear and foreboding (Ps. 56:3, 4, 11). But through prayer David regains his confidence in God. Panic gives way to the calm composure of trust (Ps. 56:3-4, 8-11).

Of interest to us is the fact that part of David's confidence is rooted in the reality that God knows everything about his circumstances and catches each falling tear in His bottle (Ps. 56:8). In Persia and in Egypt, tears were wiped from the cheeks of the mourner and carefully preserved in a tear bottle. In ancient Persia, when a sultan returned from battle, he checked his wives' tear catchers to see who among them had wept in his absence and missed him the most. Tear bottles have been found in many of the ancient tombs of Egypt and elsewhere throughout the East. These bottles were made of alabaster since glass was not yet in use. This powerful image points to God's concern for David.

God sees our falling tears and is not indifferent to them (Ps. 39:12; 2 Kings 20:5). Some years back my mother called me to tell me that God had wonderfully saved her sister Margaret after many years of persistent praying. My mum went on to say that she had shed many a tear for her prodigal sister, but God had kept those tears in His bottle, and had now answered her heart's cry.

Listen! Until God wipes away our tears in heaven, He will lovingly catch them in a bottle (Rev. 21:4). God is not unmindful or unmoved by the tears we shed (Ps. 116:8). Take the handkerchief of Psalm 56:8.

God, thank You that You care about and collect my tears now,
but will wipe them away for good later.
Comfort me with this message in a bottle.
In Jesus' Name, amen.

It Could Be Worse

Through the Lord's mercies we are not consumed, Because His compassions fail not. They are new every morning; Great is Your faithfulness.

(LAMENTATIONS 3:22-3)

John Hooper, Bishop of Gloucester, one of the lesser lights among the English reformers, was burned at the stake on February 9, 1555 under the ruthless reign of 'Bloody Mary'. He had a reputation for personal holiness and Spirit-filled preaching. Thousands came, friend and foe, to watch him burn. Along the way to his gruesome death, friends pleaded with him to recant, telling him, 'Life was sweet, and death was bitter.' To those sentiments, John Hooper gave this memorable reply: 'Life is sweet, and death is bitter, but the life to come is more sweet, and the death to come more bitter.'[1]

In these words, John Hooper reminds us that however cruel our circumstances may be and however dire the situation, it could be worse – a lot worse. As he himself so firmly grasped, we could be without the comfort of the gospel, facing life without God, and death without hope (Eph. 2:12). We could be on the broad road that leads to everlasting destruction (Matt. 7:13). We could be among those for whom this life is all the good they will ever know (Luke 16:25). But we are not! Because of God's mercy through the Cross of Calvary, we are not consumed (Lam. 3:22-3). We have not been given what our sins deserve. In the gospel, and because of Christ, God has not rewarded us according to our iniquities (Ps. 103:8-10). Quite the opposite, we have been lavished with all kinds of spiritual blessings in Christ (Eph. 1:3-14). And as the death of the brave John Hooper would show us, it is in these things that we greatly rejoice, though we may have to suffer for a while (1 Pet. 1:3-9; esp. v. 6). True contentment and peace amidst the pressing, perplexing, and painful circumstances of life comes by comparing what we have or have not to what our sins deserve. Instead of God's wrath, we

---

1. Tim Chester, *The Ordinary Hero* (Nottingham, UK: Varsity Press, 2009), p. 208.

have God's love. Instead of a hell in our future, we have heaven. The next time we feel sorry for ourselves, we need to remind ourselves that we are doing better than we deserve. We may not have all we desire, but we have more than we deserve. It could always be worse.

In his book, *The Art of Contentment*, the Puritan Thomas Watson makes this telling statement: 'Whatever change and trouble a child of God meets with, it is all the hell he shall have. Whatever eclipse may be upon his name or estate, I may say of it, as Athanasius said of his banishment, that it is a little cloud, which will soon blow over; and then his gulf is crossed, his hell is past. Death begins a wicked man's hell, but it puts an end to a godly man's hell. Think to yourself, "What if I endure this? It is but a temporary hell." Indeed, if all our hell is here, it is an easy hell.'[2] Thomas Watson is reminding us that it could be worse, but for us the best is yet to come. Death begins a wicked man's hell, but it puts an end to a godly man's hell. The bitter death is theirs, while the sweeter life is ours. It is more than a cold comfort to know that it could be worse!

God, thank You that I am doing better than I deserve.
Give me a reality check that it could be worse.
In Jesus' Name, amen.

---

2. Thomas Watson, *The Art of Contentment* (Grand Rapids, MI: Soli Dei Gloria Publications, 2008), p. 97.

Best of All

'Behold, the virgin shall be with child, and bear a Son, and they shall call His name Immanuel,' which is translated, 'God with us.'

(MATTHEW 1:23)

John Wesley was a tireless servant of God and a man who had little use for leisure time. Across his lifetime, this eighteenth-century English evangelist planted churches, established orphanages, opposed slavery, wrote books, and trained and ordained preachers. He was constantly on the move, stopping only to preach two or three times a day. In the last fifty-two years of his life, it is estimated that he preached more than 40,000 sermons. In his wake, he left behind a Methodist movement that has across history influenced tens of millions of Christians worldwide. The secret to his momentous ministry is perhaps best summarized in his last words. Just before he died in his eighty-eighth year, Wesley reportedly sat up, looked at his loved ones weeping at his bedside, and calmly said, 'Best of all, God is with us.'

God with us is indeed a great Christian and Christmas truth – a truth bound up in the name given to the Lord Jesus Christ at his birth. In final fulfillment of Isaiah 7:14, Jesus was to be called 'Immanuel' for He was in the fullest sense 'God with us' (Matt. 1:23). In the birth of Christ, the invisible God was made visible. In the birth of Christ, the Ancient of Days was born in time. In the birth of Christ, the highest being became a lowly creature, and the source of life, a dying man. In Jesus Christ the man, we have incarnate deity, the Godhead veiled in flesh (Phil. 2:5-11). As Matthew Henry the Puritan commentator puts it: 'By the light of nature, we see God as a God above us; by the light of the law, we see God as a God against us; but by the light of the gospel, we see Him as Immanuel, God with us, in our own nature, and in our interest.' In Jesus Christ, we have the bringing of God and man together both in His person and work. In His person, Christ is God miraculously manifest in flesh (1 Tim. 3:16). Through His work on the cross, Jesus makes possible the reconciliation of God and man by means of His atoning death (Col. 1:19-23). As the God-man dying for man, Jesus Christ proves to be an able and adequate mediator between God and man (1 Tim. 2:5).

Christ is God with us, and because of Christ God is for us, not against us (Rom. 8:31). We can die without fear because there is no condemnation to those who are in Christ (Rom. 8:1, 33-4). We can live without fear, for absolutely nothing, neither things present nor things to come, will separate us from God's love in Jesus Christ (Rom. 8:31-9). In fact, God is not far from each one of us. (Acts 17:27). God is with us when He seems far from us as in the case of Job. God is with us when others have forsaken us as in the case of David. God is with us in our disobedience as in the case of Jonah. God is with us when we are where we do not want to be as in the case of Joseph. God has had only one forsaken Son, and because of Him we will never be forsaken (Heb. 13:5-6; Matt. 27:45-6). Remember, best of all, God is with us!

God, best of all, You are with me.
Let that calm and cheer my soul.
In Jesus' Name, amen.

Good Grief

But I do not want you to be ignorant, brethren, concerning those who have fallen asleep, lest you sorrow as others who have no hope.

(1 Thessalonians 4:13)

Working through the grief that comes with the loss of a friend or loved one is no easy thing. In terms of stress tests, the death of a child or spouse tops the list. It is hard to go back to living after the death of someone we love. The regrets of yesterday and the fears of tomorrow make it hard to go on with today. In grieving we can be overcome with a sense of loss and loneliness, which cripples our ability to cope. One's desire to live can die the death of a thousand cuts.

Yet despite those common feelings and fears associated with grief, it is possible to express 'good grief' – the kind of grief that begins to live with the memory of the loss, but not its pain! Paul advocates this kind of grief in his counsel to the Thessalonians. In addressing their heartache over the passing of those near and dear to them, Paul encourages them to sorrow as others, but not like others (1 Thess. 4:13). Their grief was not to be hopeless (1 Thess. 4:13). Their sorrow must not give the impression that death has the last word. Christ will have the last word when He returns a second time to call living and dead saints home to heaven (1 Thess. 4:16-17). The sadness they felt, was to be tempered by the thought that while death may hide, it couldn't divide. Christians who have been separated by death will be together someday with the Lord forever, which is a great comfort (1 Thess. 4:17-18). And because of this blessed hope, Christian grief is to be limited (Titus 2:13; 1 Pet. 1:3). The grieving Christian must not hit the pause button on life, because hope in Christ drives and draws them forward to a glorious future. Vance Havner, a Southern Baptist preacher of another generation, said something after the death of his beloved wife of thirty-six years that reflects this balancing act of sorrowing, but not without hope. He said, 'I am still in the valley, but thank God, I am going through it; I am not wallowing in it.'

How does one avoid wallowing in grief? Let me suggest several things that will help the brokenhearted to express good grief:

First, practice your theology. Apply the truths of God's sovereignty, the hope of the resurrection, the comfort of the indwelling Spirit, the promise of heaven, and the sufficiency of God's grace to your situation. Work at bringing your faith and emotions together. Take control of your thoughts and bring them into captivity to Christ and His word. Second, don't deny your feelings and allow yourself to be honest with God in prayer. But remember as you talk to Him, while it is all right to ask questions of God, it is never right to question God. It is the Lord's right to give and take away (Job 1:21; Deut. 32:39). Third, extinguish any bitterness towards God or others. Don't let the sun go down on your anger (Eph. 4:26). Submit to God and reconcile with others. Fourth, commit yourself to growing and staying active. In the face of death, number your days and apply your heart to wisdom (Ps. 90:12). Fifth, allow grief to fulfill love. After his wife, Joy, died, C. S. Lewis found that for the first time he could love her in truly unselfish ways. Part of that involved setting aside his grief, and rejoicing in the gain that heaven was for her (Phil. 1:21).

God, You are my hope!
Help me to grieve well in light of these realities.
In Jesus' Name, amen.

Lost in the Dark

Oh LORD, God of my salvation, I have cried out day and night before You.

(PSALM 88:1)

Life can bring us to some very dark places – places where faith is faint, courage is absent, and hope is in short supply. This was certainly the experience of Adoniram Judson, the nineteenth-century Baptist missionary to Burma. His labors for Christ in establishing the gospel in Burma involved blood, sweat, and tears. It took him ten years to master the Burmese language. He endured twenty-one months of imprisonment. He wrestled with forces other than flesh and blood. And he lost his wife and little daughter to sickness and death within the space of six months. With the passing of his wife and child, he entered the dark night of the soul. At one point he dug his own grave and sat staring into it. On October 24, 1829, the third anniversary of his wife Ann's death, he would write: 'God is to me the Great Unknown. I believe in Him, but I find Him not.'[3]

Lost in the dark was the experience of Adoniram Judson, and he is not the only one. In reading Psalm 88 we are introduced to a musician named Heman the Ezrahite, whose life seemed to be composed of some very dark and depressing notes (88:5-6, 10-12, 18). This lament psalm is unlike so many others because it never rises to end on a happy note. It is rather dismal throughout! This man's troubles are like an endless series of waves (v. 7). The psalmist, whose life seems to have been marked by illness and trials from his earliest days, complains that his prayers for relief and good health have gone unanswered (vv. 13-18). This psalm is nothing but a bank of thick clouds. There is no sunshine, nor rays of emerging hope. It is not the kind of psalm you would be quick to read for a spiritual pick-me-up.

Yet a double take on Psalm 88 might cause us to reconsider! Ironically, does not its hopelessness offer us hope? Paradoxically, do we not find encouragement in the fact that it is full of

---

3. Daniel L. Akin, *10 Who Changed the World* (Nashville, TN: Broadman & Holman Publishers, 2012), p. 24.

discouragement? Life can be that dark! I have more than a sneaking suspicion that God included this psalm in the Psalter to let us know that He sees us in the dark and our laments do not offend Him. His love and understanding outlast our complaints! Whatever the darkness is, it is not beyond the reach of redemption or the embrace of providence. Like the psalmist we must keep on praying and trusting in the dark because God is present when He seems absent (Ps. 88:1-2, 9, 13).

If we go back to the story of Adoniram Judson, God would eventually shepherd His servant through that valley of deep darkness to brighter days. Looking back, Judson would say of those dark days: 'There is a love that never fails. If I had not felt certain that every additional trial was ordered by infinite love and mercy, I could not have survived my accumulated sufferings.'

In the dark places and spaces of life, we need to remember that there is a love that never fails – a love that was demonstrated by Christ's death amidst the darkness of Calvary (Rom. 5:8). In bearing our sin, Christ experienced the deepest darkness and the most awful sense of abandonment (Matt. 27:45-6). Christ was forsaken in the darkness that we might never be forsaken (Heb. 13:5). In the darkness, the Christian finds a silhouette of the cross, which speaks of a love that never fails.

Lost in the dark? Find your way to a God who has experienced the dark, and works in it!

> *God, thank You for not hiding in the darkness.*
> *Help me to find You when I feel lost.*
> *In Jesus' Name, amen.*

Take Shelter

The name of the LORD is a strong tower; the righteous run to it and are safe.

(PROVERBS 18:10)

Martin Niemoller was a former U-boat captain, Lutheran pastor, and one of the founders of the Confessional Church, which opposed the nazification of German Protestant churches. In 1934, Adolf Hitler summoned German church leaders to his Berlin office to bludgeon them into submission. According to Hitler, they were to confine themselves to church matters and leave the running of the country to him. Niemoller protested and reminded Hitler that he had a God-given right and duty to speak the whole truth to the church as a whole. Hitler listened in silence, but his later actions spoke loud and clear. Within hours, his Gestapo raided Niemoller's rectory and within a few days a bomb exploded in his church. It wasn't long before this brave Lutheran was arrested and imprisoned. On the day of his trial on February 7, 1938, fear pointed its cold bony finger into Niemoller's face, causing him to shudder with anxiety. As he walked through underground tunnels to the courthouse, he worried about his family, his flock, and his future! Unnerved, he climbed the steps to the courthouse with a thumping heart and troubled mind, but then he heard a whisper. At first he didn't know where it came from, but he soon realized that the attending officer was breathing into his ear the words of Proverbs 18:10: 'The name of the Lord is a strong tower; the righteous run to it and are safe.' Niemoller's fears melted away as the truth of that verse strengthened him for the trial of that day as well as the trial of his years in Nazi concentration camps.

People in the ancient world took shelter from their enemies, and sometimes the elements, in fortified positions or strong towers. These were safe places and spaces that afforded people a greater sense of security. Taking that image, the wise writer of Proverbs 18:10 encourages God's people to take shelter from life's threatening storms in what we know to be true about God, as revealed in His name or names. In Hebrew culture, a name was not a mere label, but a kind of index to the character of the person. Names reveal something about people and that is especially true of God. Therefore, when studying God's names, we see who He is and what He does, and we take shelter and find peace in those truths about God. When we run in our minds to those truths, our fears are chased away.

Here are some truths about God revealed in His names that will help chase our fears away. God is Jehovah-Ra'ah, our shepherd (Ps. 23:1). God is Jehovah-Jireh, our provider (Gen. 22:14). God is Jehovah-Shalom, our peace (Judg. 6:24). God is Jehovah-Rapha, our healer (Exod. 15:26). God is Jehovah-Tsidkenu, our righteousness (Jer. 23:6). God is Jehovah-Nissi, our banner of victory (Exod. 17:15). And God is Jehovah-Shamah, our ever-present companion (Ezek. 48:35). What great truths indeed! And as we factor them into our calculations about life, our present seems more secure and our future less daunting. As Martin Niemoller entered that Nazi courtroom, he also entered the strong tower of God's promised presence and powerful protection.

Wherever life takes us, we must always take that extra step and believe what we know to be true about God as revealed in His names.

God, I praise Your Names! I take shelter under Your cover.
In Jesus' Name, amen.

Forget About It

Joseph called the name of the firstborn Manasseh: 'For God has made me forget all my toil and all my father's house.' And the name of the second he called Ephraim: 'For God has caused me to be fruitful in the land of my affliction.'

(GENESIS 41:51-2)

Three sisters, ages ninety-two, ninety-four, and ninety-six, lived together. One night the first sister filled the bath. She put one foot in and then paused. 'Was I getting in the tub or out of the tub?' she shouted to her sisters. The second sister yelled back, 'I don't know. I will come up and see.' She started up the stairs but stopped on the first step, shouting, 'Was I going up the stairs or coming down?' The third sister was sitting at the kitchen table having tea, and heard the entire goings on. She shook her head and said, 'I sure hope I never get that forgetful', and knocked on the wooden table for good measure. Then she hollered to her sisters, 'I'll come up and help you both as soon as I see who's at the door.'[4]

Forgetfulness is natural, and comes to most of us with the passage of time. The older we get, the harder we have to work to remember birthdays, appointments, and where we left our reading glasses. But while there is a forgetfulness that is natural and imposed, there is also a forgetfulness that is necessary and voluntary. There is a forgetfulness that each of us must choose and cultivate throughout life if we are to excel in life – forgetfulness in regards to the pain and problems that others have caused us. There can be no moving forward in life if we are a prisoner to the past. There is no living to be done in the graveyard of yesterday's heartaches and headaches.

If anyone would teach us this vital lesson in successful living, it would be Joseph. His tragic yet triumphant story in Egypt is told in the book of Genesis chapters 37–50. Before his exaltation, Joseph had been cruelly betrayed by his brothers (37:1-35), falsely accused by his master's wife (39:1-20), and unjustly forgotten by

---

4. Craig Brian Larson and Phyllis Ten Elshof (eds), *1001 Illustrations that Connect* (Grand Rapids, MI: Zondervan, 2008), p. 9.

Pharaoh's butler (40:21-3). Yet God took all those dark threads and wove them together into an amazing tapestry of divine accomplishment and action. Joseph eventually became the Prime Minister of Egypt and saved his father's house from famine (45:1-15; 50:20). God, in all his glorious wisdom and sovereignty had caused him to be fruitful in the land of his affliction, as the name of his second son Ephraim shows (41:52). And alongside the gift of fruitfulness, there was the gift of forgetfulness, as borne out in the name of his first son, Manasseh.

God had caused Joseph to forget all his toil and trouble (41:51). Comforted by the truth of God's abiding presence and amazing providence, Joseph put the past behind him! His past wounds were healed in believing that God never wastes our sorrows, but works *all* things together for our good (Rom. 8:28). Just as Joseph took off those prison clothes and laid aside the hurts of the past, so we need to 'put off' malice and anger and 'put on' a new attitude of faith and love in Christ (Eph. 4:20-32; Col. 3:1-17).

God, You are the God who gives joy in the mourning
and in the morning.
Help me to put away my past, put off resentment,
and put on Christ.
In Jesus' Name, amen.

Surviving
the Struggle to Trust God
for What You Need

Having Enough

The LORD is my shepherd; I shall not want.

(PSALM 23:1)

Many years ago Dr Joseph Parker, a contemporary of C. H. Spurgeon and pastor of the famous City Temple Church, mounted the steps to his pulpit and announced his reading for the morning as Psalm 23. Slowly and distinctly he read: 'The Lord is my Shepherd; I shall not want.' There was a long pause and then closing his Bible he said, 'That is enough.'

We can all benefit from dwelling on that simple, but profound thought for a while. Those who have God as their Shepherd shall not want and will not fear (Ps. 23:1, 3). They enjoy the two things that every human heart desires, namely, sufficiency and security. Given the greatness and limitlessness of God, we shall not want because there is no lack in God's ability to take care of us in every situation (Eph. 3:20). There is little that we need other than God Himself. The person who has God for his treasure has all things in One, and that is why Paul could say that he had nothing, yet possessed everything (2 Cor. 6:10).

But how do we explain those troubling occasions when genuine needs seemingly go unmet? There are a few possibilities:

First, we have expected too much from God and too little from ourselves. We have failed to appropriate that which is available to us through harder work and greater ingenuity. God's commitment to us is not an excuse for laziness or impractical faith. God's provision for Elijah was both supernatural and natural. There were the ravens *and* also the brook (1 Kings 17:4). Elijah was not to ignore that which was within his reach.

Second, we have not made our needs sufficiently and repeatedly plain to God in prayer (James 4:2). James tells us bluntly that our lack is often a result of our failure to ask. God's promises are not only to be believed, but prayed.

Third, we fail to realize that God intends to meet our need, but just not now. While we fear the prospect of the problem getting bigger, we must remember that it will never get larger than God's ability to handle it. In fact, God often waits so He can do something greater. Jesus didn't go to Lazarus right away and heal a sick man. He waited that He might go and raise a dead man (John 11:1-44).

Fourth, we sometimes misinterpret our need and ask for something that is not good for us. The promise of Scripture is that God withholds no good thing from those who walk uprightly. Therefore, one might conclude that when He does withhold something, it is because the thing we desire is not as good as we might think (Ps. 84:11). God gives His best to those who leave the choice with Him.

God, You are sufficient.
Help me to see Your good response to my needs.
In Jesus' Name, amen.

You Are Being Followed

Surely goodness and mercy shall follow me all the days of my life; And I will dwell in the house of the LORD Forever.

(PSALM 23:6)

During the fall of 1974, President Gerald Ford's son, Michael Ford, along with his wife Gayle, attended Gordon-Conwell Theological Seminary in the Boston area. Because his father occupied the Oval Office at the time, Michael had to have two Secret Service agents with him at all times. They tried to look like students, but their cover was blown. For one thing, most of the agents were chain smokers. Since no one was allowed to smoke in classes, they were often seen taking turns leaving the class to get a nicotine fix. Whenever Mike and Gayle would take walks, two men would invariably be seen stumbling behind them. This led some at Gordon-Conwell to remark that the Secret Service men reminded them of David's words in Psalm 23:6: 'Surely goodness and mercy shall follow me all the days of my life.' So a section of the student body at the school nicknamed the two men 'Goodness' and 'Mercy'![1]

While the sons and daughters of sitting American presidents are guarded round the clock by Secret Service agents, it is nothing in comparison to the glorious truth that the children of God are shadowed day and night by God's goodness and mercy. Wherever life takes us or whatever life takes from us, we are as God's family always in the company of His goodness and mercy. Wherever we are, there they are. Goodness is there for every step and mercy is there for every sin. The word 'follow' carries the idea of being pursued. This word is used of Pharaoh's malicious pursuit of the fleeing Israelites back in the book of Exodus (Exod. 14:4). Interestingly, David the author of Psalm 23, spent most of his adult life being pursued by his enemies and God's enemies, but he found comfort in the truth that God's goodness and mercy were always hard on his heels (Heb. 13:5-6). By implication God's goodness and mercy will run after us, find

---

1.   Christy Wilson, *More to Be Desired than Gold* (Grand Rapids, MI: Color House Graphics, 1992), p. 168.

us, and minister to our needs wherever we are. We will never be bereft of God's love (Rom. 8:35-9).

God's goodness speaks of the many gifts that He showers upon His creation and church. It is all that makes life bearable and beneficial (Acts 14:17). God's goodness crested in the gift of His Son as our loving Savior (Titus 3:4-7). God's mercy alternatively speaks of God's goodness coming out to us despite our sin (Lam. 3:22-3). It is mercy that allows God's kindness and goodness to be shown. These glorious actions of God complement each other. In God's goodness we get what we don't deserve, and in God's mercy we don't get what we do deserve. It's not goodness alone, for we are rebels in need of clemency. It's not mercy alone, for we need many things beside forgiveness. In the one, we have provision for all our needs, and in the other, we have pardon for all our sins. Therefore, as a child of God, don't be afraid to step out into an unknown future, because you are being followed by God's goodness and mercy.

God, thank You that You are both good and merciful.
Let the fact that I am followed ease and edify my spirit.
In Jesus' Name, amen.

You'll Get It When You Need It

Let us therefore come boldly to the throne of grace, that we may obtain mercy and find grace to help in time of need.
(HEBREWS 4:16)

Corrie ten Boom was a Dutch Christian who, along with her father and sister, courageously hid Jews in their home during the Second World War. Her family was betrayed and handed over to the Germans, and they were sent to the notorious Ravensbruck concentration camp. During her time there, Corrie lost both her father and sister. In spite of her loss, however, she did not lose her grip on God. When she finally was released from the camp due to a clerical error, she would reflect on the fact that God had given her the strength to endure and supplied His sufficient grace as she needed it.

In fact, Corrie had learned to trust God in the midst of death early on in life. When she was a young girl, she witnessed the death of a baby and was confronted with the fragile nature of life. Spooked by this experience, she burst into tears and sobbed to her father, 'I need you. You can't die! You can't!' Seeking to comfort and counsel his frightened daughter, Corrie's father sat down beside her and gently said, 'Corrie, when you and I go to Amsterdam, when do I give you the ticket?' She sniffled a little, and replied, 'Why, just before we get on the train.' 'Exactly,' her father responded, 'and our wise Father in heaven knows when we are going to need things too. Don't run ahead of Him, Corrie. When the time comes that some of us will have to die, you will look into your heart and find the strength you need, just in time.'[2]

Corrie ten Boom learned something that day that would hold true throughout her life. God doesn't give us grace for the future. Grace cannot be stored. It must be used for the moment we are in and nothing more. Grace is like the manna that God supplied the Israelites in the wilderness. It has an expiration date on it. Its shelf life is one day (Exod. 16:21). Grace is for right now (2 Cor. 12:9).

---

2. James Emery White, *A Travelers Guide to the Kingdom* (Downers Grove, IL: Inter-Varsity Press, 2012), p. 157.

In Hebrews 4:16, we are encouraged to come boldly to the throne of our gracious God to receive mercy and find grace to help us in a time of need. A more literal rendering of that last phrase would be, 'grace for a well-timed help'. There is grace for what we need, when we need it. Now that is beautiful! Grace, not sooner, not later! Grace, no more, no less! Grace perfectly timed, and perfectly tailored.

Like Corrie ten Boom, it is easy to let our minds run ahead of us, causing a stampede of fear. It is natural for us to wonder about tomorrow, but God has promised strength for each day (Deut. 33:25). There is no grace for tomorrow until tomorrow. One of the secrets to successful living is living each day in the moment of God's sufficient and surprising grace.

Timing is everything, even when it comes to God's grace.

God, thank You that You give grace when I need it.
Help me to rely on You day by day.
In Jesus' Name, amen.

That's Not All

And of His fullness we have all received, and grace for grace.

(JOHN 1:16)

Roland Hill was an English preacher of yesteryear who loved to bring the love of God to the poor and the struggling of London. On one occasion he was given a rather large sum of money to help support the pastor of a church in a low-income area. Thinking that the amount was too much to send in one lump sum, he decided to send it in stages. Each week Roland Hill sent a portion of the gift with a note that simply said, 'More to follow!' Within a few days, the pastor received another envelope containing the same amount of money with the same message, 'More to follow.' Then there came a third, and then a fourth. In fact they continued with regularity, always accompanied by those comforting and cheering words, until the entire sum had been exhausted.

C. H. Spurgeon, the great London Baptist, loved to repeat that story to illustrate the fabulous fact that the good things we receive from God always come with the same prospect of more to follow. He said: 'When God forgives our sins, there is more forgiveness to follow. He justifies us in the righteousness of Christ, but there is more to follow. He adopts us into His family, but there is more to follow. He prepares us for heaven, but there is more to follow. He gives us grace, but there is more to follow. He helps us in old age, but there is still more to follow.' Spurgeon concluded: 'Even when we arrive in the world to come, there will still be more to follow.'

'More to follow!' That is a wonderful truth. God's grace toward us in Christ is incessant and inexhaustible. It comes in waves without abatement. 'Grace upon grace' is how the apostle John puts it (John 1:16). We might better understand that verse as saying, 'grace in the place of grace'. To help grasp what John is saying, imagine yourself standing on the bank of a fast flowing river. You fix your attention on one spot on the river, perhaps the spot right beneath your feet. As the river flows past, you see water replacing water, in constant action. It is a case of water being followed by more water. That is the picture and the promise of John 1:16. God gives more grace when we need it and how we need it (James 4:6). By trusting in Christ through the gospel, the Christian is supplied by streams of mercy that never cease (Isa. 66:12)! God's mercies are gloriously new every morning (Lam. 3:22-5).

Here is a great truth to live and die by. The faucet of God's grace will never drip or run dry. Therefore, we need to remind ourselves that God can do immeasurably more for us than we can imagine (Eph. 3:20). He wants us to be more than conquerors through His love (Rom. 8:31). He wants us to be bolder in our witness for Christ (Acts 9:22). He wants us to bear more fruit (John 15:2; Rev. 2:19). He wants us to know that where sin abounds, grace does much more abound (Rom. 5:20-1).

When we think we have exhausted God's favor, remember there is more to follow. When we think we have written our last chapter, remember there is more to follow. Because of Christ, we enjoy life, then eternal life. We experience earth, then heaven. We walk by faith, and then faith will give way to sight. There is always more to follow (Prov. 4:18; Rev. 21:4; 22:5)!

God, thank You that You are full to overflow.
Help me to expect Your constant supply.
In Jesus' Name, amen.

Sitting Pretty

Blessed be the God and Father of our Lord Jesus Christ, who has blessed us with every spiritual blessing in the heavenly places in Christ, just as He chose us in Him before the foundation of the world, that we should be holy and without blame before Him in love, having predestined us to adoption as sons by Jesus Christ to Himself, according to the good pleasure of His will, to the praise of the glory of His grace, by which He made us accepted in the Beloved.

(EPHESIANS 1:3-6)

For many years Dr Donald Grey Barnhouse occupied the prominent pulpit of the Tenth Presbyterian Church in Philadelphia. On one particular Sunday morning, a twelve-year-old boy sitting in the gallery was all-ears as the great preacher spoke about God's treatment of our sin. As Barnhouse closed out the sermon, he did so in his familiar manner by collecting many of the great promises of God's Word into one impressive sentence. As he nailed home God's treatment of our sin he said: 'Our sins are forgiven, forgotten, cleansed, pardoned, atoned for, remitted, covered; they have been cast into the depths of the sea, blotted out as a thick cloud, removed as far as the east is from the west, cast behind God's back.' Finishing his sermon, Barnhouse went to the front door of the church building to greet those attending. As he stood talking to several congregants, the twelve-year-old boy who had listened intently from the balcony tugged on his sleeve and said, 'Good sermon, Doc! Gee, we're sure sitting pretty aren't we?'

Sitting pretty is as good a way to describe the Christian's position in Christ as any. In fact, in his letter to the Ephesians, Paul talks about the Christian sitting pretty with Christ. In chapter two, Paul states that Christians are seated with Christ in the heavenly places (Eph. 2:6). Following His death and resurrection, Christ was exalted to the right hand of God, and there He sits in triumph, having achieved atonement, having conquered death, having stripped the kingdom of darkness of its power (Eph. 1:20-1). Through union with Christ, believers enter into that victory and are seated with Christ in the heavenly places, so to speak. His triumph through the cross is our triumph securing for us many things. Those many things are detailed wonderfully for us in the doxology of chapter one. Ephesians 1:3-14 is one long sentence in the Greek. Paul can hardly take a breath while telling the Ephesians how God has blessed them with every spiritual blessing in the heavenly places in Christ. This lofty and lengthy sentence screams praise to God and calls Christians to revel in God's grace toward them. Blessed by the Father, seated with Christ and indwelt by the Spirit, the Christian sure sits pretty. The Father through Christ has chosen us (vv. 3-4), adopted us (v. 5), accepted us (v. 6), redeemed us (v. 7), forgiven us (v. 7), informed us (vv. 8-10), enriched us (vv. 11-12), sealed us (v. 13), and assured us (v. 14).

The theme of Ephesians is about the wealth of blessings we enjoy seated with Christ. By implication we can walk and stand for Christ (Ch. 4–6) because we are seated with Christ (Ch. 1–3). If we take an example from the Song of Solomon, Christ has in the gospels invited us to His banqueting hall and therefore, His banner over us is love (Song 2:4). Christ in the gospel has spread a table before us in the presence of our enemies (Ps. 23:5).

Sit down today and appreciate afresh what it means to be seated with Christ. We are abundantly blessed. God's interest in us stretches from eternity past to eternity future. The Trinity Himself loves us in that the Father blesses us through His glorious Son, and that blessing is guaranteed in the gift of the indwelling Holy Spirit (Eph. 1:3-14). Listen! We can stand up to life knowing that we are seated with Christ!

God, thank You for such a bounty of blessing. Help me to
remember my privileged position in Christ.
In Jesus' Name, amen.

True to Form

By faith Sarah herself also received strength to conceive seed, and she bore a child when she was past the age, because she judged Him faithful who had promised. Therefore from one man, and him as good as dead, were born as many as the stars of the sky in multitude – innumerable as the sand, which is by the seashore.

(HEBREWS 11:11-12)

On one occasion a church leader in Melbourne, Australia, introduced the well-known missionary James Hudson Taylor to a congregation as 'our illustrious guest'. No one including the Presbyterian moderator who introduced him was ready for the first sentence of Taylor's response, 'Dear friends, I am the little servant of an illustrious Master.' Despite his many years and effective ministry in China, Hudson Taylor never saw himself as a spiritual giant, but as a weak man who was able to do great things for God because he could count on God being with him. His was a life of unwavering faith in the faithfulness of God. Writing about missions and ministry he once said, 'Want of trust is at the root of almost all our sins and all our weaknesses, and how shall we escape it but by looking to Him and observing His faithfulness.' He continued, 'The man who holds God's faithfulness will not be fool-hardy or reckless, but he will be ready for every emergency.'[3]

In these words Hudson Taylor reminds us that counting on God's faithfulness ought to subtract from our worries and add to our confidence. It makes us ready for every emergency because we can reckon on God being with us. In addition, knowing that God is always true to form helps shape our expectations. In Hebrews 11:11-12 we find Sarah, and by implication Abraham, expressing an audacious faith in God. They unwaveringly and unswervingly believed that God would be faithful to the promise He made regarding a future son (Gen. 17:19; Rom. 4:18-21). In reading their story we see the bold belief of a hundred-year-old

---

3.   Warren Wiersbe, *Walking with Giants* (Grand Rapids, MI: Baker House Books, 1976), p. 61.

man and ninety-year-old woman, who laughed in the face of the incredulous, and hoped against hope (Rom. 4:18). And of note to us is that their expectation was rooted in the faithfulness of God. Sarah 'judged Him faithful who had promised' (Heb. 11:11). Sarah and Abraham were convinced that God would do what He said He would do (1 Thess. 5:24). They rested their hope of a promised son on the utter reliability of God. They did not turn from this hope because they believed there is no shadow of turning with God (James 1:17). Clearly, this faith in the faithfulness of God was based on a moral assessment of the character of God. They believed they could count on the faithfulness of God because, firstly, God is perfect and does not deteriorate, secondly, God is immutable and does not change, and thirdly, God is omnipotent and is able to do all that He promises. Like Hudson Taylor, they held to the faithfulness of God and it held them during testing times.

In a world of broken promises, dashed dreams, undependable people, and ever changing circumstances, it is a glorious thing to be able to root our confidence and anchor our hopes in the faithfulness of God (1 Thess. 5:23-4; 2 Tim. 2:11-13). The God of the Bible doesn't change, doesn't lie, and doesn't disappoint. His faithfulness is everlasting (Ps. 119:90), fixed (89:2), unfailing (89:33), infinite (36:5), great (Lam. 3:23), and incomparable (Ps. 89:8). What a wonderful truth to know that each morning we can rely on God's patience, provision, forgiveness, and love.

No matter how we feel, we can bank on the fact that God will be true to form.

God, thank You that You will always be true
to your perfect form.
I can depend on You in all circumstances.
In Jesus' Name, amen.

Great Expectations

Now to Him who is able to do exceedingly abundantly about all that we ask or think, according to the power that works in us, to Him be the glory in the church by Christ Jesus to all generations, forever and ever. Amen.

(Ephesians 3:20-1)

First Lady of American Theatre, Helen Hayes, once told a story of her attempt to cook her first Thanksgiving turkey. Although not much of a cook and after several years of marriage, she committed to try and prepare her own turkey for the festive holiday. Knowing this would come as a bit of a shock to her husband and son, she sat them down and said, 'This may not come out exactly the way you want it to. If it is not a good turkey, don't say a thing. Without any comment, just stand up from the table, and we'll go to the nearest restaurant and eat.' Some time later, Helen walked into the dining room with the turkey only to find her husband and son already standing with their coats and hats on. The boys weren't taking any chances![4]

As Helen Hayes's husband and son demonstrate, our expectations affect and direct our conduct. What we see happening next tends to shape what we do next. What we think is possible tends to control what we are willing to try. I think we all would admit that expectations play a very important role in life, for they either limit us or liberate us. To expect much allows us to lean forward into the day believing the best is yet to come. To expect little has us on our heels and wondering if our best days are behind us. Expectations set the mood in life. They either fuel optimism or feed pessimism.

For the Christian, expectations ought to be sky high because we believe in a God who is able to do exceedingly, abundantly, above all that we can ask or think according to the power that works in us (Eph. 3:20-1). Throughout chapters one through three, Paul has been leading the Ephesians on a journey of discovery regarding the abundant riches of God's grace and glory (Eph. 1:7, 18; 2:7; 3:16; 3:8). In this final majestic view of

---

4. *On This Holy Night* (Nashville, TN: Thomas Nelson, 2013), p. 2.

God and the unsearchable riches of Christ, Paul reminds the Ephesians and us that our expectations ought not to be bound by human reason or resources because God, in His omniscience and omnipotence, exceeds human reason and resources. God is able to do what we think cannot be done. God is able to supply in abundance what in our lives is in short supply. According to Paul, God's ability exceeds our comprehension and God's abundance exceeds our multiplied needs. God is able to do all, above all, abundantly above all, and exceedingly abundantly above all!

Talk about God's abundance: God's pardon is abundant (Isa. 55:7). God's kindness is abundant (Neh. 9:17). God's blessings are abundant (Ps. 65:11). God's peace is abundant (Jer. 33:6). God's Spirit is abundant (Titus 3:5-6). God's irrepressible hope is abundant (1 Peter 1:3-4). And God's gift of life in Christ is abundant (John 10:10). Christians ought to be people of great expectations! Yet, the sad thing is that we often lack this kind of expectation. I think we can all say with the English preacher John Jowett: 'What I have asked for is as nothing compared to the ability of God to give. I have asked for a cupful, and the ocean remains. I have asked for a sunbeam, and the sun abides. My best asking falls immeasurably short of my Father's giving. It is beyond all that we can ask.'

Let's expect more from life by expecting more from God!

God, I praise You for being an abundant God.
Help me to expect more from You.
In Jesus' Name, amen.

Surviving
the Struggle to Defeat Temptation and the Tempter

The Temptations within the Temptation

Jesus said to him, 'It is written again, "You shall not tempt the LORD your God."'

(MATTHEW 4:7)

The story is told of man with a bulging waistline who decided to do something about his weight. Engaging the fight with the flab, he decided to change his route to work so that he would not pass his favorite doughnut shop. He was so committed to this fight to lose weight that he told his coworkers of his stand against the lure of doughnuts. But not long after sharing this in the office, he arrived at work one morning with a big box of doughnuts. When his surprised coworkers asked what was going on, he said, 'These are no ordinary doughnuts. They're from the Lord.' 'What in the world are you talking about?' they asked. The man replied, 'It's quite simple. Today on my way into the office I accidentally drove by my favorite doughnut shop and saw all those glazed and sprinkle topped doughnuts calling my name from the window. I knew I had to pray for deliverance and strength, so I said, "Lord, if you want me to have one of these delicious doughnuts, You are going to have to give me a parking space right in front of the doughnut shop. If this happens I know that you want me to have some doughnuts." And sure enough, after eight trips around the block, there was a parking place right in front of the doughnut shop!'[1]

Although funny, this story does point to the serious matter of not being serious about temptation. In our struggle against the rulers of the darkness, we tend to fight with kid gloves. Our resolve to do right and fight wrong often has the consistency of Jell-O. Instead of taking cover and finding God's way of escape, we put ourselves knowingly and wantonly in the line of fire (1 Cor. 10:13; Prov. 7:6-27). Like Samson who foolishly fell asleep in the lap of Delilah, we often expose ourselves to unnecessary spiritual danger (Judg. 16:18-20). This is what I would call the temptation within temptation, and that temptation is to test

---

1.   Tony Evans, *Life Essentials* (Chicago, IL: Moody Press, 2003), p. 205.

God. Jesus taught us in His own temptation of this temptation to test God (Matt. 4:5-7). In refusing to leap off the pinnacle of the Temple in Jerusalem, Jesus recognized not only that Satan was twisting the Scripture from Psalm 91:11-12, but, also that God is not committed to saving us from foolish actions. We test God when we are not sincere in our attempts to obey His Word. We test God when we knowingly put ourselves in harm's way and expect God to rescue us.

Listen, we cannot pray to God to deliver us from evil while at the same time leading ourselves into temptation (Matt. 6:13). We cannot be claiming the promises of God while acting disobediently (Deut. 6:16-17). Placing oneself in the way of sin is a matter tempting God and delighting Satan. God comes to those who flee from sin into His arms (Gen. 39:12, 21, 23; 1 Cor. 6:18; 1 Tim. 6:11)! Those who would not sin and test God must not sit at the door of temptation!

God, I thank You that You tempt no man.
Help me to stay as far away as possible from temptation
and come running to You when it knocks at my door.
In Jesus' Name, amen.

Our Own Worst Enemy

Remember therefore from where you have fallen; repent and do the first works, or else I will come to you quickly and remove your lampstand from its place—unless you repent.

(REVELATION 2:5)

In January of 1967, three American heroes, Gus Grissom, Ed White, and Roger Chaffee, perished in the first great tragedy to hit the infant American space program. The crew of Apollo 1 was busy conducting preflight tests when an electrical spark triggered a flash fire in the oxygen rich environment of the space capsule. There was no escape for the three men as the door to the capsule was sealed by a complex series of interlocking latches that took ninety long seconds to open in ideal circumstances. In retrospect the tragedy seemed preventable and so the Congress called for hearings on the matter. Colonel Frank Borman, himself an astronaut, took the stand to testify and said, 'It was a lack of imagination.' In those words, Borman was pointing to the fact that the NASA engineers focused too much on the threats to the astronauts from the outside – threats such as the fires of reentry and the cold of outer space. But they had stopped short of asking, 'What if a fire breaks out in the oxygen-saturated space capsule before takeoff?' They considered the real threats were from the outside and not the inside.[2]

The mistake made by the NASA engineers is a mistake that can be repeated in businesses, homes, and churches all across America. It is a failure to appreciate the threats that lie close at hand. Disaster can result from a self-inflicted wound, as much as anything else. We can be our own worst enemy. Our own sins, stupidity, and slackness can ruin businesses, destroy families, and immobilize churches. It is interesting to note in Jesus' letter to the church at Ephesus that He sees their greatest threat as lying inside, not outside (Rev. 2:4-5). While they were ministering in a hostile environment, it was not the hatred of the world that

---

2. Blaine McCormick and David Davenport, *Shepherd Leadership* (San Francisco, CA: Jossey-Bass, 2003), p. 121.

posed the greatest danger, but their lack of love for Christ. It was their cold attachment to Christ that threatened their vitality and future. According to Jesus, unless they repented, God's judgment would bring an end to the church at Ephesus in the removal of their lampstand (Rev. 2:5). Sin within the church was the real threat, not wickedness within the society.

The church in America today is fixated on what is happening outside and the threats posed by a culture increasingly marked by neo-paganism and post-modernism. But Jesus would remind us that we can imperil ourselves by neglecting the inside threats of formalism (Rev. 2:4), false doctrine (2:14), sexual immorality (2:20), spiritual pretense (3:1), and nominalism (3:15-16). 'Beware of no man more than of yourself; we carry our worst enemies within us,' Charles Spurgeon rightly said. We have seen the enemy and he is us! The church needs to call itself to repentance (Rev. 2:5, 16, 21, 3:3, 19). The church's future lies not in reforming society, but in reforming itself. Let judgment begin in the house of God (1 Pet. 4:17)! It is only a repentant church that can survive, and win an unrepentant world.

*God, thank You for Your reminder that my sin poses
the real threat.
I come to You for reformation of self.
In Jesus' Name, amen.*

Another Attack is Coming

Now when the devil had ended every temptation, he departed from Him until an opportune time.

(LUKE 4:13)

In 1984, British Prime Minister Margaret Thatcher narrowly escaped with her life after two bombs exploded in the Grand Hotel in Brighton, England, where she was staying along with many other government figures. They were there for the national conference of the Conservative Party. The IRA, an Irish Republican terrorist group, had left the bombs. They sadly killed five people and injured many others. Mrs Thatcher was still awake when the bomb went off at 2:54 a.m. She had been working on her conference speech at the time. The bomb shredded through her bathroom barely two minutes after she had left it. The IRA claimed responsibility the next day, promising to try again. Their statement out of Dublin included these now famous, and chilling words: 'Today we were unlucky, but remember we only have to be lucky once. You have to be lucky always.' Chilling words indeed!

Just as Mrs Thatcher had to face the ongoing and deadly threat of IRA terrorism, which she did with great fortitude, so the Christian faces the interminable threat of our archenemy Satan (James 4:7). Each day requires that we put ourselves on notice of the danger he poses to our walk with Christ and our work for Christ (1 Pet. 5:8). He is always looking for that vulnerable moment, that season in life, when he can take a clean shot at our spiritual life in Christ. In Luke 4:13, we see him leave the Lord Jesus after the temptation in the wilderness with the intent of re-engaging his battle with Christ at a more opportune time. Satan works on the principle that if at first you don't succeed try, try again. Luke tells us that his departing from Christ was for the sole purpose of reloading. Satan operates just like an IRA terrorist in that he lies in wait for the right moment to strike again with deadly force. Satan carefully chooses his moment to attack.

Reflecting on that caused me to think about those certain times and seasons when the enemy might chance his luck.

Number one, during the time of one's conversion just like the Thessalonians (1 Thess. 1:5-6; 3:4-5). Number two, during a time of sickness and suffering just like Paul (2 Cor. 12:7-10). Number three, during a time of physical exhaustion just like Christ (Matt. 4:1-3). Number four, during a time of notable spiritual blessing just like Peter (Matt. 16:13-20, 21-3). Number five, during a time of idleness and lack of vigilance just like David (2 Sam. 11:1-4; cp. 1 Pet. 5:8). Number six, during a time of spiritual pretense just like Ananias and Sapphira (Acts 5:1-3).

Look! Satan is not a trigger-happy gangster, but a patient sniper. He waits for the best moment to pull the trigger. We must put on our spiritual armor and watch with all prayer (Eph. 6:10-18). Remember, eternal vigilance is the price of liberty. Satan, that spiritual terrorist, has only to be lucky once. We have to be lucky all the time. Don't give him a next time.

God, I worship Your holiness and detest Satan's schemes.
I pray for vigilance.
In Jesus' Name, amen.

United We Stand

Having disarmed principalities and powers, He made a public spectacle of them, triumphing over them in it.

(COLOSSIANS 2:15)

In biblical times the Roman Army was a fierce and formidable force to be reckoned with. Julius Caesar had invaded Britain in 55 B.C. with only 10,000 men. Despite being outnumbered four to one, he had beaten the Gallic tribes of France at the battle of Alesia three years earlier. Everyone in the Roman Empire knew that the strength of the Roman Army lay not in its numbers, but its discipline. A united army doesn't need to be a large army to be victorious. While the barbarians tended to rely on numbers and mob tactics, the Roman generals drilled their legionaries to form a disciplined 'triple line'. If charged by cavalry, they could adopt a 'square' formation. If bombarded by a hailstorm of arrows, they could adopt the 'tortoise' formation behind a united wall of shields. If the generals and legionnaires saw an opportunity to advance in battle they could reorder into a 'wedge' formation that galvanized the soldiers' strength, allowing them to punch holes in the enemy lines. The Roman Army reminds us of the abiding truth that united we stand, and divided we fall.[3]

Interestingly, the image of a Roman battalion standing with their shields locked in united opposition against the enemy is one that Paul draws upon to remind the church of the importance of Christian unity in the battle against the world, the flesh, and the devil. While writing to the Colossians, Paul says: 'For though I am absent in the flesh, yet I am with you in the spirit, rejoicing to see your good order, and the steadfastness of your faith in Christ' (Col. 2:5). The phrase 'good order' speaks of an unbroken military line, a solid front. The Colossian church was like a well-organized army showing a united front against the false teachers who sought to diminish the sufficiency and supremacy of Christ (Col. 2:1-10). In Ephesians six, Paul calls upon the Christians in that city to take a stand against the underworld of the devil and his demons (Eph. 6:10-18).

---

3.   Phil Moore, *John* (Oxford, UK: Monarch Books, 2012), p. 221.

Of note is the fact that the word 'you' throughout this passage is in the plural. Spiritual warfare is essentially a corporate act. The book of Ephesians headlines the fact that through our reconciliation to God, those who are in Christ have been reconciled to one another. There is one body, one faith, and one Father of all (Eph. 4:4-6). The walls that divide us have been torn down through what Christ did on the cross (Eph. 2:14-18). We have been made one in Christ and have equal access to our Father (Eph. 2:18).

In the context of spiritual warfare, Christian unity is a powerful weapon. A redeemed and reconciled Christian community is a glorious reversal of Satan's work of cosmic disruption and disharmony. A harmonious community of Christians signals the triumph of the gospel and is a harbinger of God's future plan to bring all things in heaven and on earth together under the Lordship of Christ (Eph. 3:10-11; 1:10).

The Christian faces an axis of evil in the world around, the flesh within, and the devil below. The odds are against us. But the path to victory lies not in our numbers, but in our disciplined love for each other and labor together. May we be on guard in endeavoring to keep the unity of the Spirit (Eph. 4:1-3)! May we close ranks and give the devil no room to work with bad attitudes or actions among us (Eph. 4:25-33)!

God, thank You that You are a God of unity.
I pray that the church would rally together with You at the front.
In Jesus' Name, amen.

Speak of the Devil

And the LORD said to Satan, 'Behold, all that he has is in your power; only do not lay a hand on his person.' So Satan went out from the presence of the LORD.

(JOB 1:12)

During the Second World War, C. J. Auchinleck, the commander-in-chief of the Middle East Force on the Allied side, put out the following order:

> There exists a real danger that our friend Rommel is becoming a king or a magician or a bogeyman to our troops who are talking far too much about him. He is by no means a superman, although he is undoubtedly very energetic and able. Even if he were a superman, it would be highly undesirable that our men should credit him with supernatural powers. I wish to dispel by all possible means that idea that Rommel represents something more than the ordinary. The more important thing now is that we do not always talk of Rommel when we mean the enemy in Libya. We must refer to the 'Germans' or 'the Axis powers' or 'the enemy' and not always be harping about Rommel. Please ensure that this order is put into immediate effect, and impress upon all commanders that, from a psychological point of view, it is a matter of the highest importance.[4]

That is an order that needs to be adapted and applied to every soldier of the cross engaged in spiritual warfare. While our adversary the devil is formidable, intelligent, crafty, and resourceful, he is not omniscient, omnipresent, or omnipotent. We must not play into his hands by making him a greater villain than he is. We must be sober and proportionate in our judgment of him, which involves recognizing what he can do, but also what he cannot do (1 Pet. 5:8). Satan is an angelic being, an awesome being, an adversarial being, but he also is an accountable being. The opening chapters of Job set before us this revealing and refreshing truth that the devil is not autonomous or sovereign.

---

4. Steve Brown, *When Your Rope Breaks* (Grand Rapids, MI: Baker House Books, 1988), p. 153.

He is not running amuck across the earth with no one to rein him in, impede his devilish schemes, or challenge his existence. He is not above God as he once wished, but before God as a subject before his king.

His limitation is to be seen on a number of fronts within the drama of Job: one, in his summons to appear before God with the rest of the angelic host (Job 1:6; 2:1), two, in the fact that he cannot touch or harm Job because of God's protection (1:10), and three, in the reality that even when he is given permission to mess with Job, there are boundaries set by God (1:12; 2:6). The biblical text is clear that Satan is on a leash, and that leash is in the grip of God's sovereign hand. As Martin Luther said, 'The devil is God's devil.' Think about it! The opening chapters of Job show us that even in his acts of disobedience Satan must obey God. While Satan can act outside the moral will of God, he cannot act outside the sovereign will of God. There is no dualism in the Bible. God and Satan are not duking it out to see who comes out on top. God rules and overrules (Ps. 115:3; Dan. 4:26)! Jesus was victorious on the cross (Col. 2:13-15). Satan's doom is sure (Matt. 25:41; John 16:11; Rev. 20:10).

When speaking of the devil, let us make God great, Jesus pre-eminent, and the devil small. To make Satan more than he is, is to diminish God before men, weaken the gospel's triumphant message, and bring undue fear to the ranks of God's people. Make it your habit to get up each morning mindful of the fact that there are two great forces at work in this world: the unlimited power of God and the limited power of Satan!

God, I marvel that You are even sovereign over Satan. Help me
to think much more of You than of him.
In Jesus' Name, amen.

Weapons at the Ready

And take the helmet of salvation, and the sword of the Spirit, which is the word of God.

(Ephesians 6:17)

On May 26, 1941, a little known event took place that proved to be a game changer in World War II. The German submarine U-566 was returning from a killing spree against allied merchant ships when a lookout spotted two large warships on the horizon. After crash driving at the command of Lieutenant Wohlfarth, the U-boat came a bit later to periscope depth to find that it was strategically placed between the two enemy warships. It was the stuff war dreams were made of. In front of U-566 was the British battle cruiser *Renown*, and to their rear was the British aircraft carrier *Ark Royal*. Wohlfarth could see biplanes on the *Ark Royal* readying themselves for take-off. It was the perfect set up. All the Germans had to do was fire torpedoes from both ends, and both enemy vessels would be crippled or sunk. The only problem was, U-566 had no torpedoes! They were out of ammo! Their torpedoes had been used up in their hunt for allied merchant ships. To rub salt into the wound, little did the crew of U-566 know that one of the planes on the flight deck of the *Ark Royal* would drop ordinance an hour later that would badly damage the rudder of the famous German battleship, the *Bismarck*. Sitting dead in the water due to its inability to maneuver, the *Bismarck* became a sitting duck for the British Navy to pound and sink the next day. Historians tell us that the sinking of the *Bismarck* with a loss of almost 2,300 men was a pivotal moment in World War II. If only U-566 had carried more torpedoes![5]

The spiritual counterpart to this story is the believer's failure to arm themselves through Bible study and memorization for spiritual warfare. In Ephesians 6:17 Paul tells the Christian to urgently take up the sword of the Spirit, which is the Word of God, in the fight with our adversary the devil. Tested and

---

5. Robert Daniels, *The War Within* (Wheaton, IL: Crossway Books, 2005), p. 221.

tempted by the evil one, the Christian must have his Bible at the ready so that he can fight the devil's lies with God's truth (John 8:44b; John 17:17).

Of note to us, is the fact that in the New Testament, two Greek words are used to translate 'the Word' of God. The first is a familiar Greek word *logos*, which speaks of the complete and replete revelation of God. The second and lesser-known word is *rhēma*, which connotes a particular statement or saying in the Bible that applies directly to a given situation. Interestingly, the word *rhēma* is the term used in Ephesians 6:17. In other words, Paul is telling us that when we find ourselves toe to toe with the enemy, we need to be able to handle the Scriptures with skill and specificity. We need to be able to immediately draw from the wisdom of God's Word for that specific situation. A wide and working knowledge of the Bible provides the Christian with a spiritual armory from which to draw weapons and ammunition in the fight for our purity and progress in Christ (Ps. 119:9).

In the temptation of Christ in the wilderness, we see the Lord Jesus handle the Scriptures purposefully and precisely. As Satan assaults Him, His defense against each slimy solicitation was a verse from the book of Deuteronomy that particularly contradicted the devil's deceptions (Matt. 4:4, 7, 10; Deut. 8:3; 6:16; 6:13). Jesus wielded the sword of the Spirit with deftness and directness. He drew from the Old Testament, reminding us that the Old and New Testament are in harmony (2 Tim. 3:16). Both Testaments validate each other and are there for our encouragement and edification (Rom. 15:4). Therefore, Bibles at the ready must be the believer's watchword if we are to win this war against evil and turn the tide for good.

God, thank You for the weapons You have shared with me.
Help me to use them as they were meant to be used.
In Jesus' name, amen.

Run for Your Life

Be sober, be vigilant; because your adversary the devil walks about like a roaring lion, seeking whom he may devour. Resist him, steadfast in the faith, knowing that the same sufferings are experienced by your brotherhood in the world.

(1 PETER 5:8-9)

In his book *Born to Run,* Christopher McDougall says this: 'Every morning in Africa a gazelle wakes up, it knows it must outrun the fastest lion or it will be killed. Every morning in Africa a lion wakes up, it knows it must run faster than the slowest gazelle, or it will starve. It doesn't matter whether you're the lion or the gazelle when the sun comes up, you'd better be running.'

On the plains of Africa, passivity is a killer! Not to do something is to have something done to you. If the gazelle fails to run, it gets eaten. If the lion fails to run, it has nothing to eat. Both the gazelle and lion must run for their life literally. And so it is with the Christian. By way of comparison, the apostle Peter warns the Christians of the Dispersion that when the sun comes up they had better be on their toes for their adversary 'the devil walks about like a roaring lion, seeking whom he may devour' (1 Pet. 5:8). The Christian's nemesis, the devil, is always sniffing around trying to pick up the scent of the lazy Christian, the prayerless saint, and the unbelieving believer who fails to understand the spiritual danger they are in each day. Therefore, passivity in the Christian life is just as deadly as it is on the plains of Africa. Scripture teaches that those who quickly give up the fight (1 Tim. 6:11-12), those who do not watch and pray (Mark 14:37-8), and those who do not put on the armor of God every day (Eph. 6:10-18) are easy pickings for Satan, the adversary of our souls.

In fact, Peter identifies four spiritual stragglers that are most vulnerable to the attacks of Satan, the prowling lion. First, he would remind us that the cocky Christian is in danger (1 Pet. 5:5). Pride, a lack of dependence upon God was Satan's sin, and when it is found in us, gives the devil more room to work (1 Tim. 3:6). Second, Peter would remind us that the anxious soul is at risk (1 Pet. 5:7). At the heart of anxiety is a divided mind, a mind that cannot fully trust or obey God. Satan likes to wedge himself there bringing accusations and spreading lies (Rev. 12:10; John 8:44). Third, the apostle would remind us that the sleepy-headed are a target (1 Pet. 5:8). Vigilance is the price of spiritual liberty. To snooze is to lose. The Christian is not and ought not to be ignorant of Satan's schemes (2 Cor. 2:11). Fourth, and finally, Peter would remind us that the spiritual pacifist is a sitting duck for the enemy (1 Pet. 5:9). It is never the case that if you leave the devil alone he will leave you alone. He is actively seeking our spiritual destruction. Consequently, he must be resisted aggressively through prayer, theological conviction, Christian community, and dependence upon Christ (James 4:7).

Regarding these last two vulnerabilities, George Malone insightfully writes: 'The lion can only devour what he has overtaken, or what has purposely lain down. Passive acceptance of our circumstance or our sin is permission for the devil to take more ground. The passive man or woman is a person who has lost all hope that any effort will make a difference.'[6] That is a good word! Don't accept your circumstance or sin. Run for your life! Run looking to Jesus (Heb. 12:1-2)!

God, thank You that You are the object of my faith.
Help me be on the offensive with You!
In Jesus' Name, amen.

---

6.   George Malone, *Arming for Spiritual Warfare* (Downers Grove, IL: Inter-Varsity Press, 1991), p. 100.

Surviving
the Struggle to Witness Boldly

Up Close and Personal

He first found his own brother Simon, and said to him, 'We have found the Messiah' (which is translated, the Christ). And he brought him to Jesus

(JOHN 1:41-2)

What is the best way to reach the world for Christ? The answer to that question is one home and one heart at a time! Evangelism that is up close and personal is still the best method of reaching the lost. Statistics continue to show that a majority of people come to Christ through the personal witness of a Christian pointing them to Christ. Public preaching has its place within evangelism, but it is a bit like taking a bucket of water and throwing it over a number of open-necked bottles; whereas personal evangelism, the one-on-one kind, is like taking each bottle to the tap and filling it. The great Baptist preacher C. H. Spurgeon used to say, 'Hand-picked fruit for me every time!'

One of the great examples of this approach to winning the world is Andrew the disciple. He is not as prominent as some of the other disciples in the biblical record, but when he does come out of the woodwork of the gospels, we find him doing one thing and one thing only, and that is introducing people to Christ. Andrew was happy to simply be a signpost pointing people to the only way to God. He was always bringing people to Christ. In John 1:40-2 he brings his own brother Peter to Christ. In John 6:8-9 he brings a boy to Christ. In John 12:20-2 he brings some Greeks to Christ. In fact, he was so good at this that when those Greeks approached another disciple Philip about seeing Christ, Philip naturally thought of Andrew as the best one to introduce them to Christ. Here was a man noted for introducing people to Christ. Andrew may have lived to some degree in the shadow of his brother Peter, who was off winning souls to Christ by the thousand as on the day of Pentecost (Acts 2:38-42). He is often described as Simon Peter's brother (Matt. 10:2-4; John 6:8), but it must not be forgotten that it was Andrew who found Peter. It was the little fisherman who landed the big fisherman.

You may not see yourself as a Peter, but you can be an Andrew. You can be the kind of person who each and every day by life and lip points others to Christ. You can be the kind of person who offers a hand to those who are reaching out to God!

An old man, walking the beach at dawn, noticed a young man ahead of him picking up starfish and flinging them back into the sea. Catching up with the youth, he asked him what he was doing. The answer was that the stranded starfish would die if left until the morning sun. 'But the beach goes on for miles and there are millions of starfish,' countered the old man. 'How can your effort make a difference?' The young man looked at the starfish in his hand and then threw it to safety in the sea. 'It makes a difference to this one,' he said.

You are a fisher of men, and Andrew reminds you that you can make a difference for Christ one heart and one home at a time.

God, thank You for using us in Your grand plan of redemption.
Help me to reach out to others with Your love.
In Jesus' Name, amen.

Living Letters

You are our epistle written in our hearts, known and read by all men; clearly you are an epistle of Christ, ministered by us, written not with ink but by the Spirit of the living God, not on tablets of stone but on tablets of flesh, that is, of the heart.

(2 CORINTHIANS 3:2-3)

Towards the end of his book, *Max on Life*, author Max Lucado encourages his readers to remember that the apostles were writers, and that we need to pick up the pens that Paul, John, and Luke have set down. The pen is indeed mightier than the sword, and writing is a wonderful, and often overlooked avenue for a wider ministry for Christ. Well-written words can change lives and travel to places far beyond our own travels. Plus, when someone buys a book, they are inviting the author to join them in an intensely private moment. They clear the calendar, turn off the television, find an easy chair or a corner, and invite the author to talk to them one on one. That is an invitation not to be turned down. In this challenge to pick up the mantle of gospel writing, Max Lucado said something rather striking to future writers! He said: 'Let your life be your first draft. Shouldn't Christian writers be Christian writers? Love grumpy neighbors. Feed hungry people. Help a struggling church. Pay your bills, your dues, and attention to your wife. You'll never write better than you live.'[1] Lucado is reminding aspiring writers that anything they write must be prefaced by a life well-lived. The author's life is indeed the first draft of anything he or she writes.

In his second letter to the Corinthians, Paul would remind each of us that we are living letters intended to commend and communicate Christ (2 Cor. 3:1-4). God has authored a work of grace in each of our hearts and homes that others should be able to read in big bold letters (Heb. 12:2). Some imposters at Corinth had called Paul's apostolic credentials and character into question, causing Paul to fire back. Drawing upon the common practice of letters of recommendation in that day, Paul argues

---

1.   Max Lucado, *Max on Life* (Nashville, TN: Thomas Nelson, 2010), p. 233.

that his own letter of recommendation was the Corinthians themselves. The transformed lives of the Corinthians was a letter commending Paul and his ministry – a letter not written on paper, but hearts – a letter not written in ink, but one authored by the work of the Spirit through the Apostle. Surely these living letters were evidence enough to shut the mouth of Paul's critics.

What a compelling and convicting image of the Christian – a living letter written by God's own saving hand that people can read each and every day. Hopefully your life and mine are legible testimonies to God's amazing grace and transforming power. The implication of this image is that there is the gospel according to Matthew, Mark, Luke, and John, and then there is the gospel according to you – the gospel that you write each and every day by the words that you say and the deeds that you do!

D. L. Moody, the evangelist, once said, 'For some people, we are the only gospel they will ever read, and some of us need revising.' Don't forget to be God's postcard to the world today!

God, thank You for being the Author of my life.
Fill the pages of my life with a true testimony.
In Jesus' Name, amen.

Having a Fit

Therefore he reasoned in the synagogue with the Jews and with the Gentile worshipers, and in the marketplace daily with those who happened to be there.

(ACTS 17:17)

Henry Martyn was a nineteenth-century British missionary who left behind a glittering academic career at Cambridge to go to India and Persia for Christ. He was only twenty-four years of age when he left the British Isles. It took him almost a year to get there, and he was no sooner there than his health began to deteriorate. This was something he would wrestle with for several years until his untimely death at age thirty-one. Yet in that short span of time, he managed to produce translations of the New Testament in Urdu, Arabic, and Persian, which laid the groundwork for missions in that region for years to come. Throughout his troubles, travails, and trials, Martyn was driven by a burning desire to see the supremacy of Christ made known among all peoples. There is a story that comes out of his life that attests to that reality. When Martyn saw a picture of Jesus bowing down and grasping the robes of Mohammed, he responded, 'I could not endure existence if Jesus was not glorified.'[2]

Henry Martyn reminds us that missions and evangelism must be predicated upon a burning jealousy on our part for God's glory among the nations (Pss. 96:3; 97:1). There was a certain provocation that fueled his missionary endeavor and endurance. He could not live if Christ were not glorified. You see the same visceral reaction on the part of Paul as he enters the great city of Athens (Acts 17:16-17). It was a city marked by idolatry and religious pluralism, a city where it was easier to find a god than a man. Such idolatry, which robbed God of His place and Jesus of His pre-eminence, moved Paul to the core of his being. He was provoked in his spirit. In fact, in describing Paul's reaction, 'Dr' Luke uses a medical term, which describes

---

2. John Stott, *Life in Christ* (Grand Rapids, MI: Baker Books, 2003), p. 103.

a seizure or an epileptic fit. The fact that God was being robbed of the glory that was due His name gave Paul a fit.

Both Henry Martyn and the Apostle Paul remind us that Christian missions ought to be the overflow of our delight in God and the desire to see His name and fame spread throughout the earth. Fundamentally, true evangelism begins with a love for God, not a love for the lost, a passion for God not a compassion for men. We must not put the cart before the horse. Our evangelism must be God-centered before it is man-centered. We must love God, then our neighbor (Matt. 22:37-9)! The worship of God – a burning desire to see our glorious God exalted in the midst of His creation – must fuel and kindle our desire for world missions. As John Piper has rightly said, 'Evangelism exists because worship doesn't.' A failure of nerve on our part in the task of evangelism is a red flag telling us that we do not love God enough. In a world of false religions, in a world where the name of Jesus is a curse word, in a world where men worship the creature rather than the Creator (Rom. 1:25), you and I need to be provoked to more eagerly proclaim the supremacy of Jesus Christ. He alone is worthy (Rev. 5:12)!

Are you having a fit?

God, You deserve worship from the world!
Help me to proclaim Your Name that saves!
In Jesus' Name, amen.

Going Public

*Let your light so shine before men, that they may see your
good works and glorify your Father in heaven.*

(MATTHEW 5:16)

A few years back I found myself struggling in the pulpit to
project my voice with any volume. After several visits to doctors
and vocal specialists, it was determined that I had a nodule on
my vocal cord that would require surgery to remove it. As the
surgery approached, I traveled to St Johns Hopkins Medical
Center on Wilshire Boulevard in LA to meet the surgeon who
would carry out this delicate procedure. During the elevator ride
to the appropriate floor, I noticed the man opposite me in the
elevator had his head down and a baseball cap drawn over his
eyes in an attempt to hide his identity. But the more I peeked at
this mysterious individual, the more convinced I was sure he was
a famous Hollywood actor. To confirm my hunch, I subtly slid
down the elevator wall to see, and sure enough, it was Michael
Keaton who had played in such blockbuster movies as *Batman*
and *Beetlejuice*. Since it was just the two of us, I said, 'You are
Michael Keaton, aren't you?' Now that his cover was blown, the
man reluctantly replied that he was, and a pleasant exchange
pursued. I told him that I had enjoyed several of his movies.
One interesting tidbit was his surprise to find a fellow Irishman,
a Baptist pastor in Santa Clarita, and not a Roman Catholic
priest in Ireland. He exited the elevator politely before I could
explain why. For me, it was an exciting encounter because it's
not every day you get to meet a Hollywood star, but I supposed
for him it was just another interruption of his privacy by a pesky
member of the public.

Some time later while reflecting on that meeting in the
elevator, I thought about how hard it must be for celebrities
to enjoy any kind of privacy or anonymity while out in public.
They are hounded by the paparazzi and pestered by an adoring
public. But that thought then morphed into another thought.
While Michael Keaton is entitled to a private life, the Christian
is not entitled to a private faith. Our faith in the Lord Jesus Christ
must be known and shown. It belongs in the public square.

The gospel by its very nature and implication is demonstrable (Acts 26:26). By definition the Christian faith is the outliving of the in-living Christ. Jesus is our life, and that transformative reality permeates our life and ought to ooze out of every pore (Gal. 2:20; Phil. 1:21). The Christian cannot remain silent or anonymous with so great a salvation (Heb. 2:3).

We ought to go public with our faith in three ways! First, we are to go public in words (Rom. 10:9)! We must confess Jesus as Lord. We must share His gospel and defend His truth. We must declare His glory among the nations (1 Pet. 2:9). Second, we are to go public in works (Matt. 5:16). Jesus went about doing good, and so must we. Our Christian faith must be a balance of words and deeds. Let us visit the sick. Let us sit beside the lonely. Let us serve the poor. Let us fight the scourge of abortion. Third, we are to go public in water (Matt. 28:18-20). Christian baptism upon belief in Christ is another wonderful way to make Christ known. In the symbolism of immersion into and out of water, we preach the gospel of new life in Christ.

Listen! The greatest threat to Christianity is not communism, secularism, or militant Islam; it is Christians trying to get to heaven incognito. Michael Keaton is entitled to a private life; we are not entitled to a private faith (Matt. 10:32-3). Are you going public?

God, Your value compels me to communicate with a lost world.
Help me to promote You in public as well as in private.
In Jesus' Name, amen.

Divine Appointments

The woman said to Him, 'I know that Messiah is coming'
(who is called Christ). 'When He comes, He will tell us all
things.' Jesus said to her, 'I who speak to you am He.'

(JOHN 4:25-6)

Pat and Tina O'Neal are friends of mine who have faithfully and
fruitfully served God for many years through CBMC, Christian
Business Men's Committee. Over dinner one night they told me
of a time when they found themselves stranded in Johannesburg
on the way home from a trip to Africa. Their unexpected
overnight stay was due to a missed connection outside of their
control. Instead of getting upset, they reminded themselves
that there are no accidents with God, only appointments. So
wherever they went they decided to ask people, 'Are you the
reason we are in South Africa?' One of the employees at the
hotel who was asked the question said, 'Maybe, I don't know.'
The next day, however, as Pat and Tina waited for their evening
flight home, they decided to grab a light lunch in a café near the
hotel. After their lunch had been served, the lady manager came
by to see if they were satisfied with the service they had received.
As they responded to the manager's question, they asked her
the big question, 'Are you the reason we are in South Africa?' In
God's good providence, a conversation ensued that provided Pat
and Tina a wonderful opportunity to share the gospel with this
lady. But that is not the end of the story or the best part of the
story. When the manager departed, a waitress approached the
O'Neals with tears in her eyes and shared with them that there
were a number of Christians in the business praying intently for
their manager's salvation. Not wanting to get fired or upset their
manager unnecessarily, they had been praying that God would
make a way for them to share the gospel with her. From their
perspective, that prayer had just been answered, and Pat and
Tina had just discovered the reason they were in South Africa.

Surely this story is a reminder that with God there are no
accidents only appointments. It is also a vivid reminder that
nothing is left to chance when it comes to how and when a person
comes to faith in Christ. That is the testimony of Scripture.

Salvation is of the Lord! It is His gift to give, and the circumstances that led to that event are also of the Lord (Jonah 2:9; Rev. 7:10). We see that demonstrably in the conversion of the Samaritan woman who meets Jesus at the well of Sychar, and takes from Him the living water of the gospel (John 4:1-42). This woman's salvation was divinely orchestrated. First, Jesus did not have to pass through Samaria on His journey from Jerusalem to Galilee. There were alternative routes open to Him, but He took that particular path (John 4:4). Second, Jesus arrives at the well around noon, just in time to meet the woman (vv. 6-7). This woman had a checkered past marked by public scandal, and so she comes alone to fetch water at the hottest part of the day. What a coincidence? No, what providence! Third, the disciples arrive back just in time to witness the woman leaving to tell her friends about Christ (vv. 27-9). Jesus bids them to open their eyes to the gospel opportunities that are unfolding all around them (vv. 30-8). They were in a God-appointed place, at a God-appointed time, to be reapers in a God-appointed harvest.

In relation to salvation God is the chief evangelist. Don't miss your divine appointment today in sharing the gospel! Somebody is the reason you are where you are.

God, thank You that You purposefully organize my encounters.
Help me to be aware of the divine appointments
around me today.
In Jesus' Name, amen.

I Like the Way You Look

*... not pilfering, but showing all good fidelity, that they may
adorn the doctrine of God our Savior in all things.*

(TITUS 2:10)

Ravi Zacharias tells the story of an evangelist named Yakov,
a story he borrowed from a book entitled *Of Whom the World
Was Not Worthy,* written by Marie Chapian. The story goes that
Yakov had been witnessing to an older man by the name of
Cimmerman, but his efforts to win this man to Christ were met
with stiff resistance. When Yakov talked about the love of Christ,
Cimmerman talked of his hatred for Christians. He talked of the
hypocrisy of some priests that he knew and how they cloaked
their inconsistent lives with clerical vestments. Yakov paused,
and then asked Cimmerman to imagine a situation in which his
coat, trousers, and boots were stolen and then worn by a man
who robbed a bank. The police saw the man from a distance, but
were unable to apprehend him. Carrying on with the imaginary
story, Yakov described a scenario that had the police coming
to Cimmerman and accusing him of robbing the bank. Before
Yakov could say much more, Cimmerman stopped him and
asked him to leave. He knew where he was going and what he
was doing through the story. He understood that Yakov was
saying that Christ couldn't and shouldn't be blamed for the
actions of those who pretend to act in His name.

Yakov did leave Cimmerman that day, but he sought to live
the love of Christ before him each and every day after that. As
time went by, Yakov's Christian life was so compelling and so
attractive that Cimmerman approached Yakov and asked him
how he might commit his life to Jesus Christ as Savior and Lord.
Cimmerman said to Yakov, 'Thank you for being in my life. You
wear His coat very well.'[3]

Making the gospel attractive by the way we live and love is
something that God calls all Christians to do. God wants us,
in every way that we can, to make the teaching about God our

---

3. D. A. Carson (ed.), *Telling the Truth* (Grand Rapids, MI: Zondervan,
    2000), p. 42.

Savior appealing and alluring. He wants us to put on a show of glamorous godliness that catches the attention of the world. In his letter to Titus, Paul underscores this when he calls upon the Christian slaves on the island of Crete to adorn the doctrine of God before their masters through honest, trustworthy, and respectful behavior (Titus 2:9-10). Interestingly, the Greek word for 'adorn' gives us our English word *cosmetics*. It was used in that day to speak of the advantageous and attractive arrangement of jewelry. By implication, Paul is calling them to live in such a way that the gospel is made attractive by their attitudes and actions. In fact, one of the dominant themes of this letter is exemplary Christian behavior for the sake of those still outside of Christ (Titus 2:5, 7, 8, 10, 11; 3:1, 8). Against the background of a rotten and rotting culture, Paul calls the Christians on Crete to put the beauty of the gospel and the sweetness of Christ on display each day and in every way (Titus 1:12). The grace of God that had appeared in Christ was now to be manifested in them (Titus 2:11-12). They were to be a pattern of good works (Titus 2:7, 14; 3:1, 8, 14).

One of the greatest apologetics for the Christian faith is faithful Christians who wear the coat of Christ well. The world is watching us, and I hope they like what they see.

God, You are altogether lovely.
Help others to see Your loveliness in my life.
In Jesus' Name, amen.

Every Hour of Every Day

I beseech you therefore, brethren, by the mercies of God, that you present your bodies a living sacrifice, holy, acceptable to God, which is your reasonable service. And do not be conformed to this world, but be transformed by the renewing of your mind, that you may prove what is that good and acceptable and perfect will of God.

(ROMANS 12:1-2)

Dr George Tiller was a committed abortionist who had a hand in the deaths of over sixty thousand unborn children, most of them late term. In 2009 he was himself killed when he was gunned down at, of all places, his church. He was shot in the side of the head during a worship service in a Lutheran church where he served as an usher. One of Tiller's fellow congregants was quoted as saying, 'The church has stood behind Dr Tiller,' while describing him as 'a Christian, [a] good man'. Remember, this 'good man' had ended the lives of thousands of unborn and defenseless children. The staggering implication of the congregant's words regarding Dr Tiller is that they saw no incongruity or inconsistency between being a church usher on a Sunday and an abortionist on a Monday.[4]

The story of Dr Tiller is a gross example of something that we all need to guard against, and that is separating acts of worship on a Sunday from our behavior and lifestyle the rest of the week. True faith is an active thing. It is a life-transforming principle. It gives shape and substance to all that we are and all that we do (Gal. 2:20; James 2:18; Heb. 10:38). It is a grave error to think that isolated acts of worship can make up for a life out of sync with God (Matt. 15:8). One's liturgy on the weekend and one's life on weekdays cannot be divorced; they must be married (1 Sam. 15:22-3). If our lives are false throughout the week, our worship can never be true on Sunday. A life that is disconnected from the will of God makes worship an insult to God (Isa. 1:10-17).

---

4. Voddie Baucham Jr., *Family Shepherds* (Wheaton, IL: Crossway Books, 2011), p. 159.

In light of this danger of separating life and liturgy, work and worship, how critical is Paul's admonition in Romans 12:1-2? Here Paul appeals to the Christians in Rome. In the face of God's mercy shown to them in Christ, they are to present their bodies as 'living sacrifices, holy and acceptable to God'. This was their reasonable service. This was their logical worship. Reason and logic tell them and us, as Jonathan Edwards would later put it: 'If God loves the whole person, then the only fitting response is to return the whole person to that love, to offer our bodies as living sacrifices.'

Also, in making his case, Paul reminds every Christian that living for Christ each and every day is logical, and not only that, but is integral to a life that pleases God. The trueness of our worship cannot be properly judged by one hour on a Sunday, but by every hour of every day. Worship takes in all of life; there is no wall between the sacred and the secular. In fact, in Romans 12 and 13 the apostle Paul outlines what worship looks like throughout the week by underscoring Christian behavior in relation to certain relationships. This apostolic worship checklist focuses on (1) how you relate to yourself (Rom. 12:3, 3-8); (2) how you relate to fellow believers (vv. 10, 9-16); (3) how you relate to your enemies (vv. 17, 17-21); (4) how you relate to secular authorities (13:1, 1-7); and, (5) how you relate to Christian standards (vv. 13, 8-14). All of life is an act of reasonable worship because He is blessed forever (Rom. 9:5). Therefore we cannot sing like angels on a Sunday and live like devils on a Monday, and expect God to say, amen!

God, You are God every day of the week!
Help godly form to be my norm.
In Jesus' Name, amen.

Surviving
the Struggle to Move Forward and Embrace the Future

Going Forward

I do not count myself to have apprehended; but one thing I do, forgetting those things which are behind and reaching forward to those things which are ahead, I press toward the goal for the prize of the upward call of God in Christ Jesus.
(PHILIPPIANS 3:13-14)

Some years back, the *Reader's Digest* magazine told the story of Athletic Director Frank Howard's response to a suggestion someone made that rowing become part of the Clemson University's athletic program. Howard declared, 'We are not gonna have no sport where you sit down and go backwards.'

In God's work and in the Christian's life, there is to be no going back either. This was certainly the passion and perspective of the Apostle Paul as he wrote to the church at Philippi, reminding them that just as the Olympic runner does not look back over his shoulder but presses forward with every available ounce of energy toward the finish line and victory, so Christians must not linger on their way to heaven (Phil. 3:13-14). They must constantly be reaching out and stretching toward that 'upward call of God in Christ Jesus'. There must be a strenuous pressing forward into an ever deepening and joyous relationship with Christ.

And this surge forward must of necessity involve a detachment with the past. Looking back works against going forward (Luke 9:62). Paul says to the Christian that the things that are behind us must be forgotten. Forgotten not in the sense that we erase them from our memory (which is impossible), but in the sense that we are no longer influenced or affected by what is past!

First, we need to forget our past sins. Paul himself was a man with a messy past, but he had obtained mercy and there was no looking back (1 Tim. 1:13). He wasn't going to remember what God had so gloriously forgotten through Christ (Heb. 10:17). The Christian's past before Christ must not be allowed to quarrel with the Christian's future in Christ.

Second, we need to forget our past sorrows. Paul's life and ministry was one full of trials and troubles (2 Cor. 11:23-8). He carried the scars of wrestling with people and fighting with devils, yet Paul saw no future in sitting around nursing his wounds. The Christian realizes that the cross always comes before the crown.

Third, we need to forget our past successes. Paul had a ministry resumé second to none (2 Cor. 12:11). He had planted churches, mentored leaders, and written much Scripture, but since his life wasn't done, there was more work to be done (2 Tim. 2:6-8). The Christian knows that now is not the time to polish medals, but to keep moving.

David Livingstone, who left Scotland for Africa as a missionary, said, 'I am ready to go anywhere so long as it's forward.' For the Christian there is no future in the past. Today, may we lean upon God and look to Christ as we press more deeply towards a future that grows brighter and brighter (Prov. 4:18). Get up and go forward!

God, thank You for the reminder that I am in a race.
Help me to always be pressing forward toward the goal.
In Jesus' Name, amen.

Failure is Not Final

A bruised reed He will not break, And smoking flax He will not quench, till He sends forth justice to victory.

(MATTHEW 12:20)

The God of the Bible is the God of the second chance, a God who prefers to mend rather than discard. In Matthew 12:20, it is said of our Lord Jesus that 'a bruised reed He will not break and a smoking flax He will not quench.' The reed, which was used by shepherds as a kind of flute, was immediately discarded once it cracked. A smoldering wick was also useless for giving light. These references represent those who are rejected by society at large as useless and damaged goods. But rather than 'break' or 'quench' such people, God's commitment in Christ is to mend and heal. When we land hard, Christ's nailed-pierced hand is there to help us bounce back.

So, when it comes to failure don't fail to remember the following:

First, we all fail. As the offspring of Adam and children of dust it is not hard for us to muck things up (Ps. 103:14). Abraham was a liar. Jacob was a deceiver. Moses was a murderer. David was an adulterer. Peter was a blasphemer. Morally speaking, no one has a perfect score (Rom. 3:23). The best of us are ultimately not that good.

Two, we can fail well. There is such a thing as 'failing forward' by learning from what we have done wrong, repenting, and laying hold of God's forgiveness. We can drown in guilt or we can swim back to shore helped by the incoming tide of God's grace. Elijah emerged from his failure a new man with a new mission (1 Kings 19:15-16). Peter was strengthened after his failure and set to work again by Christ (Luke 22:31-2). We must not waste our sorrows or sins. They must be allowed to temper and teach us about our sorry selves and the One who is greater than all our sin. Fail successfully.

Three, our failures do not cause God to fail. Heaven is never shaken by the stumbles of God's servants. In case you have never noticed, many of the heroes of Hebrews 11 were reclaimed failures. Abraham the liar, Jacob the swindler, Moses the murderer, and David the adulterer are all in there. Our failures, thankfully, do not tie God's hands. God is a potter and works with mud. He is able to take that which is marred and remake it into a thing of beauty (Jer. 18:1-6). God loves to restore the broken and brittle and then parade them before the world as trophies of His grace.

The great British leader, Winston Churchill, who forged new qualities in the crucible of failure, once noted: 'Success is never final and failure is never fatal; it is the courage to continue that counts.' Failure is never final unless you give up!

God, thank You that You never fail to make beauty
out of the broken.
Help me to look up to You, instead of give up on me.
In Jesus' Name, amen.

Little By Little

You shall not be terrified of them; for the LORD your God, the great and awesome God, is among you. And the LORD your God will drive out those nations before you little by little.

(DEUTERONOMY 7:21-2)

Andrew Carnegie, the great industrialist and philanthropist, once stated in a speech before a graduating class that he thought that all young men fell into three categories: those who did not do all their duty, those who only professed to do their duty, and those who did all their duty, plus a little bit more. 'It is the little more that wins,' he said, 'Do your duty and a little bit more, and the future will take care of itself.'

Do your duty and a little bit more is a good word. It is that little bit more that makes a big difference in life. Those extra few moments with the Lord as the day begins make a huge difference throughout the day. Those extra few words of kindness go a long way to keeping marriages healthy and relationships strong. Those extra few pushes get the job done. It is that little bit more that wins the day. Little by little is how we make something more of our lives, businesses, homes, churches, and relationships with God.

Along these lines, we see in the book of Deuteronomy that God's plan for the conquest of Canaan by Israel was a gradual one. God says: 'You shall not be terrified of them; for the Lord your God, the great and awesome God is among you. And the Lord your God will drive out those nations before you *little by little*, lest the beasts of the field become too numerous for you' (Deut. 7:21-2). Though God had the power to destroy Israel's enemies instantly, He chose to do it progressively. On a practical level, this approach would prevent an unhealthy accumulation of corpses and the multiplication of desolate land overrun by wild animals. But spiritually, this approach would foster an enlarged trust in God on the part of Israel. The conquest would not be smooth or speedy; Israel would have to look to God on a daily basis. Canaan would be conquered little by little. It took Israel about seven years to get control of the whole land.

Little by little, that is God's way! Instant success may actually defeat us in the long run. It is the long struggle towards eventual success that builds character, produces fortitude, tempers faith, and in the end, deepens gratitude. That which is achieved little by little within the will of God encourages faith and hope, but that which is gained quickly and easily tempts us towards independence, prayerlessness, and pride. The book of Proverbs warns against the danger of an inheritance quickly gained (Prov. 20:21). No son or daughter is well served if they are given too much, too soon. Little by little is how God wants to grow us (2 Cor. 3:18), supply our needs (1 Kings 17:15-16), and employ us (Matt. 25:21).

Listen, life is a day-by-day experience, lived and won little by little. They say that life is hard by the yard, but a cinch by the inch. Don't be impatient with God or life. Do your duty and a little bit more, and the future will take care of itself.

God, thank You for the reminder that You work progressively.
Help me to be a work in progress.
In Jesus' Name, amen.

The Past is the Past

And to the angel of the church in Sardis write, 'These things says He who has the seven Spirits of God and the seven stars: "I know your works, that you have a name that you are alive, but you are dead."'

(REVELATION 3:1)

Following his team's crushing defeat of Notre Dame 42–14 in the 2013 BCS National Championship, Nick Saban, coach of Alabama, was asked how long he planned to enjoy yet another championship. Saban replied, 'Well, two days, and we are going to start on next year.' Forty-eight hours, and then it was back to the drawing board! But those who know Saban would not be surprised by his post-game comments. A hallmark of Saban's coaching philosophy is what he calls the 24-hour rule. The team can enjoy a win on Saturday or wallow in self-pity after a poor performance for a maximum of 24 hours. Then it is back to doing the little things that make a big difference on game-day. For a coach who has won three national championships with the Crimson Tide, today is all about tomorrow, not yesterday.

As this story reminds us, every church and every Christian must guard against the clear and present danger and distraction of glorying in the past at the expense of today and tomorrow. The past is no more; it is today that counts. If the past was good, it can certainly act as a rudder, but it must never be allowed to become an anchor holding us down or back. Too many churches and Christians are dead in the water because they are living off the past or thinking of what God did in earlier years. This was evidently the problem with the church at Sardis (Rev. 3:1-6). According to Jesus, this was a church overdrawing on its past accomplishments. They were still basking in the afterglow of a glorious past. Jesus said: 'I know your works, that you have a name that you are alive, but you are dead' (Rev. 3:1).' Like the city itself this was a church that had seen better days. Sardis was a city living off its past reputation. Once the capital of the ancient Lydian kingdom, it crested in terms of its prosperity and power under Croesus in the sixth century B.C., flourished under its Persian conquerors, but then slipped into a steady decline towards obscurity. By Jesus' time, the contrast between the city's past splendor and present decline was sad and striking. This decline was now being mirrored to some degree in the church! This was a body of believers moving not from good to great, but from good to not so good. Jesus therefore calls the leadership at Sardis to halt the slippage and to strengthen the things that remain because their works were not complete before God (Rev. 3:2). Their service, worship, prayers, evangelism, and love for God and man were less than they used to be.

There is no future in the past (Prov. 4:18; Phil. 3:12-14). For the child of God, it is always a case of 'hats off to the past, and coats off to the future.' We must discipline ourselves in the light of what we have learned from the church at Sardis to make the least of what has gone and the most of what is to come. May every new day mark a new beginning of spiritual optimism and obedience in each of our lives. Surely all that we have done for Christ up until this moment better prepares us to do more in the next. Yesterday's obedience wouldn't do for today, but it should allow today's obedience to be fuller.

The past is the past; let's get on with the future.

God, thank You for what is past, but let me not depend on the past. I'm trusting You with my future.
In Jesus' Name, amen.

The Future of History

Thus says the LORD: 'Stand in the ways and see, and ask for the old paths, where the good way is, and walk in it; Then you will find rest for your souls. But they said, "We will not walk in it."'

(JEREMIAH 6:16)

Some years ago I spent a weekend in London visiting a friend from Northern Ireland. While there, friends of my friend from Welwyn Garden City Baptist Church, just outside the city, kindly offered to show us around London for the day. When they asked me what I wanted to see and where I wanted to go, I mentioned the Parliament buildings, Buckingham Palace, and Westminster Abbey. But most of all, I told them we had to find time to visit The Metropolitan Tabernacle. My final request was met with a blank stare. They inquired, 'What is The Metropolitan Tabernacle?' Their reply shocked me, since I was talking to two English Baptists. So I shot back, 'Really? It is the church where Charles Haddon Spurgeon preached!' Then things went from bad to worse. They looked at each other, and then at me, and responded, 'Who is Spurgeon?' I could not believe my ears! Here were two young English Baptists living just outside London blithely unaware of their own history.

That encounter that day reminded me and speaks to us all, about the sad fact that the church today is suffering from a severe memory loss. We see no future in our past. History is bunk! We seem to have fallen prey to a postmodern mindset that honors neither history nor heroes. A look at the modern Christian movement shows that it is wholly contemporary in its ethos and pragmatic in its practice. Ours is a generation of Christians suffering from historical amnesia, bent on a future without a past. But that is a huge mistake. The Bible never encourages us to discount God's work in the past (Pss. 77:10-11; 90:1; 105:1-6; 143:5). 'Remember' is one of God's favorite words. The Bible not only encourages us to remember God's wonderful works, but it also encourages us to memorialize the deeds of the just (Prov. 10:7). We must not forsake the faith of our fathers (2 Chron. 7:19-22; 1 Kings 9:4-9; Jude 3). This emphasis underscores why Jeremiah the Prophet urges the people of God in his day to ask for the ancient paths for they constitute the good way (Jer. 6:16). This verse reminds us to allow the streaming light of history to light the path to the future. Jeremiah is saying that the way forward is back, for the past helps us to predict and secure the future.

History is not bunk; it is critical to our future. First, history instructs us (Rom. 15:4). Times may have changed and trends may have changed, but there is nothing new under the sun (Eccles. 1:9). Men haven't changed. Satan hasn't changed. Truth hasn't changed (1 Pet. 1:25). And God doesn't change (Mal 3:6; Heb. 13:8). Therefore, history is a great tutor and teacher. History teaches us that ideas have consequences. History teaches us God's ways and Satan's schemes. Second, history inspires us (Mark 14:9; Heb. 12:1). The record of shining faith in the past acts as a shot in the arm to our own belief in God. Those who in yesteryear shipwrecked themselves on God, provide an anchor for our own faith during life's swelling tides. Third, history integrates us (Jude 3). Our common salvation reminds us that we are part of something bigger than the moment we are in. The contemporary Christian must have an ancient focus. God has been working across history, and we need to be faithful to that heritage. Listen and learn! There is no future in ignoring the past!

God, thank You for the glorious reality that You have been working for generations. Help me to respect and regard the past as I look to today and tomorrow.
In Jesus' Name, amen.

Not Now But Later

'Yet you shall see the land before you, though you shall not go there, into the land which I am giving to the children of Israel.'

(DEUTERONOMY 32:52)

The missionary Henry C. Morrison was headed home to America by boat after forty years of faithful and fruitful service in Africa. Coincidentally, President Theodore Roosevelt was traveling on the same ship following a hunting expedition to Africa. Upon their arrival in New York, Morrison became quite dejected when he compared the great fanfare the President received upon his homecoming with the absence of people to welcome him back from the battlefield of world missions. Yet, in the midst of his sulking, God seemed to speak to him in a still small voice. That small voice said, 'Henry – you're not home yet.'[1]

Not home yet! What a good reminder to those of us, who like Henry Morrison, have forgotten that in God's kingdom, it is always a case of suffering followed by glory, crosses followed by crowns, earth followed by heaven, rejection followed by recognition, and loss followed by gain (Rom. 8:17-18; 2 Cor. 4:16-18; 1 Pet. 4:12-13). This biblical truth of 'not now but later' when it comes to the Christian's reward and recognition is a timely correction to those of us who are looking for our best life now. The Scriptures are clear this world is not our home, and it must never be treated as such. To expect to find happiness here on earth will be to the Christian the cause of great unhappiness. Too many Christians have forgotten that there are two worlds, and this life is the short and nasty one (Mark 10:28-31; Acts 14:22; 1 Pet. 1:6-7). Suffering followed by glory – this is God's order, and this is basic Christianity. Our best life is not now, but later!

This thought of 'not now but later' is illustrated wonderfully for us in the life, really the death, of Moses (Deut. 32:48-52). Prior to the beginning of the conquest of Canaan, God takes Moses to the summit of Mount Nebo to survey the land promised

---

1. Michael P. Green, *Illustrations for Biblical Preaching* (Grand Rapids, MI: Baker House Books, 1982), p. 206.

to the children of Israel as a divine inheritance. Moses was to view the Promised Land, a land that he was not permitted to enter (Deut. 32:49, 52; 3:27; 34:4). The text of Deuteronomy repeatedly makes the point that Moses would see the land, but not step foot on it. At first look, this emphasis seems to be a matter of agony. Moses seeing, but not entering, is torture. At second look, however, this emphasis seems to be more a matter of anticipation. In Hebrew law, to view something communicated a legal implication. It anticipated the future purchase and possession of the land. For examples of this, read Genesis 13:14-15, Matthew 4:8-10, and Luke 14:18! That is why God told Moses to run his eye up and down and around the Promised Land (Deut. 3:27; 34:1-3). What Moses saw was his, even though he was not allowed to enjoy it in the present. He would later stand on it in the company of the Lord Jesus (Matt. 17:1-3). The Promised Land was his, not now but later.

The story of Moses surveying Canaan underscores the vital Christian principle and pattern that not everything promised to us can be immediately acquired. We live in hope. As Thomas Guthrie would remind us: 'Earth for work, heaven for wages; this life for the battle, another for the crown; time for employment, eternity for enjoyment.'

God, thank You for the reminder that my best life is later.
Help me to accept the cross before the crown.
In Jesus' Name, amen.

Not Here to Stay

*These all died in faith, not having received the promises, but
having seen them afar off were assured of them, embraced
them and confessed that they were strangers and pilgrims
on the earth. For those who say such things declare plainly
that they seek a homeland. And truly if they had called to
mind that country from which they had come out, they
would have had opportunity to return. But now they desire
a better, that is, a heavenly country. Therefore God is not
ashamed to be called their God, for He has prepared a city
for them.*

(HEBREWS 11:13-16)

An anonymous writer tells about an American tourist's visit
to the nineteenth-century Polish rabbi Hofetz Chaim. Upon
entering the rabbi's home, the guest was shocked and surprised
to find the place so sparsely furnished. The main living quarters
was a simple room lined with books, a table, and a bare bench!
The tourist asked, 'Where is your furniture?' 'Where is yours?'
replied the rabbi. 'Mine?' asked the puzzled American. 'But I am
a visitor here. I'm only passing through.' 'So am I,' said Hofetz
Chaim.[2]

Passing through is the right perspective on life. While we
are creatures of time, we are also children of eternity. In a real
sense, Christians are not citizens of earth trying to get to
heaven, but citizens of heaven trying to get through life on earth
(Phil. 3:20). Heaven to us is not just a destination or doctrine; it is
a disposition, a mindset, a way of thinking and living (Col. 3:1-3).
Heaven is our north star as we make our trek through life. Its
beauty captures our imagination, its values shape our behavior,
its endlessness redeems our time, its joys alleviate our sorrows,
and its King owns our worship. Heaven ought to be in us as
a transforming truth before we are in heaven. The Christian is
a pilgrim, Christian life a pilgrimage (1 Pet. 1:17; 2:11).

This idea of pilgrimage finds wonderful expression in the
life of the Patriarchs. Speaking of Abraham, Isaac, and Jacob,

---

2.   Green, *Illustrations for Biblical Preaching*, p. 238.

the writer to the Hebrews points to the fact that while they journeyed through this life, they did so with an eye to the afterlife (Heb. 11:13-16). Even while they lived in the Promised Land, they were looking for a better country, a country whose builder and maker was God (11:16, 10). They never felt at home in their new home. In fact, according to this epistle, the anticipation of this better country defined them as men (11:14). The thought of this future fatherland not only comforted them in death, it categorized them in life (11:13-14). By life and by lip, they made clear that they were strangers and pilgrims on the earth (Gen. 17:8; 23:4; 28:4; 47:9). While in Canaan, they had no desire to go back to Ur, but they did long for heaven, that better country (Heb. 11:15-16). Heaven was in them before they were in heaven.

This pilgrim status and alien mindset is one that should categorize us as followers of the Lord Jesus (Phil. 3:20; 1 Pet. 1:17; 2:11). Remember, the Christian life is a pilgrimage. Because we are not of this world, we march to a different drumbeat, often finding ourselves out of step with the prevailing culture (John 17:14-19; Acts 9:2). We do not live as the world while in the world because we are being drawn to another world. Our disposition is that of the pilgrim, and not the tourist. And just like pilgrims, we hold material things lightly, we take the long view on things along the way, we don't travel alone, we are constantly being drawn forward, we maintain our focus without distraction, and we are happiest at the journey's end. One early Christian document, the *Epistle to Diognetus*, described Christians as, '[Those who] dwell in their own countries, but only as sojourners ... Every foreign country is a homeland to them, and every homeland is foreign ... Their existence is on earth, but their citizenship is in heaven.'

God, thank You that I am a citizen of heaven.
Make me a pilgrim as I journey towards being with You forever.
In Jesus' Name, amen.